# Wendell Berry
## and the
# Cultivation
# of Life

········································
## A Reader's Guide
········································

# J. Matthew Bonzo
# Michael R. Stevens

**Brazos**Press
*a division of Baker Publishing Group*
Grand Rapids, Michigan

Published by Brazos Press
a division of Baker Publishing Group
P.O. Box 6287, Grand Rapids, MI 49516-6287
www.brazospress.com

Printed in the United States of America

Library of Congress Cataloging-in-Publication Data
Bonzo, J. Matthew, 1963–
    Wendell Berry and the cultivation of life : a reader's guide / J. Matthew Bonzo and Michael R. Stevens.
        p.  cm.
    Includes bibliographical references and index.
    ISBN 978-1-58743-195-1 (pbk.)
    1. Berry, Wendell, 1934—Criticism and interpretation. 2. Christian literature, American—History and criticism. 3. Production (Economic theory) in literature. 4. Work in literature. 5. Sustainable development. 6. Communities in literature. 7. Place (Philosophy) in literature. I. Stevens, Michael R. 1969- II. Title.
    PS3552.E75Z6 2008
    818'.5409—dc22                                    2008020682

Selections from *The Art of the Commonplace, Another Turn of the Crank, Memory of Old Jack, Jayber Crow, Selected Poems, A Timbered Choir, Citizenship Papers, The Way of Ignorance, That Distant Land,* and *Given: New Poems* are printed with the permission of Counterpoint Press.

Reprinted by permission of North Point Press, a division of Farrar, Straus, and Giroux, LLC: Excerpts from "In Rain" and "Satisfactions of the Mad Farmer" from *Collected Poems: 1957-1982* by Wendell Berry. Copyright © 1985 by Wendell Berry. Excerpts from "An Agricultural Journey to Peru," "Discipline and Hope," and "Native Grasses and What They Mean" from *The Gift of the Good Land* by Wendell Berry. Copyright © 1981 by Wendell Berry. Excerpts from "Higher Education and Home Defense," "Home Economics," "Looking Ahead," "The Loss of the University," and "Preface" from *Home Economics* by Wendell Berry. Copyright © 1987 by Wendell Berry.

# Contents

# Acknowledgments

In *Andy Catlett: Early Travels: A Novel*, Wendell Berry suggests that the great question to ponder at the end of one's life is if you "have been grateful enough for love received and given." We certainly have been recipients of much love and would like to respond gratefully. While the following list is by no means exhaustive, we express gratitude to the following individuals and communities: To the team at Brazos Press, especially Rodney Clapp, Rebecca Cooper, and Lisa Ann Cockrel, for their guidance. To the Civitas Center of Cornerstone University for their continuing discussions on essential issues. To our students at Cornerstone University, especially those who were in the Homelessness and Homemaking and the Home Economics classes. These classes generated the idea of this book and helped to refine our thoughts. To our kids who sacrificed some summer time with their dads as we toiled in Michael's office, and our wives, Dorothe (Matt) and Linda (Michael), who have shown us how to make a house a home. To the various groups where we presented parts of this material, including LaGrave Christian Reformed Church, First Evangelical Free Church of Grand Rapids, Abraham Kuyper Study Center of Brazil, the Swiss L'Abri, and the Notre Dame Center for Culture and Ethics. Special mention should be given to Rebecca Wolfe, Chris Allers, and Jenna Whalley who read and commented on this work.

# Abbreviations Used for Frequently Cited Texts

## (All by Wendell Berry)

ACP    *The Art of the Commonplace: The Agrarian Essays of Wendell Berry.* Ed. Norman Wirzba. Washington, DC: Counterpoint, 2002.

ATC    *Another Turn of the Crank.* Washington, DC: Counterpoint, 1996.

CH    *A Continuous Harmony: Essays Cultural & Agricultural.* New York: Harcourt Brace, 1972 (Shoemaker & Hoard, 2004).

CP    *The Collected Poems, 1957-1982.* San Francisco: North Point, 1985.

CZP    *Citizenship Papers.* Washington, DC: Shoemaker & Hoard, 2003.

GGL    *The Gift of Good Land: Further Essays Cultural and Agricultural.* San Francisco: North Point, 1981.

GP    *Given: New Poems.* Washington DC: Shoemaker & Hoard, 2005.

HC    *Hannah Coulter.* Washington, DC: Shoemaker & Hoard, 2004.

HE    *Home Economics: Fourteen Essays.* San Francisco: North Point, 1987.

HW    *The Hidden Wound.* Boston: Houghton Mifflin, 1970.

JC    *Jayber Crow.* Washington, DC: Counterpoint, 2000.

LLH    *The Long-Legged House.* New York: Harcourt Brace Jovanovich, 1969 (Shoemaker & Hoard, 2004).

LM    *Life Is a Miracle.* Washington, DC: Counterpoint, 2000.

MOJ    *The Memory of Old Jack.* New York: Harcourt, Brace, Jovanovich, 1974. (revised Counterpoint, 2001).

SEFC   *Sex, Economy, Freedom & Community*. New York: Pantheon, 1993.

SP      *The Selected Poems of Wendell Berry*. Washington, DC: Counterpoint, 1999.

TDL    *That Distant Land: The Collected Stories*. Washington, DC: Shoemaker & Hoard, 2004.

UA     *The Unsettling of America: Culture and Agriculture*. San Francisco: Sierra Club, 1977; Avon Books, 1978; Sierra Club, 1986.

WI      *The Way of Ignorance and Other Essays*. Washington, DC: Shoemaker & Hoard, 2005.

WPF   *What Are People For?* New York: North Point, 1990.

# Bibliography

(compiled by Tom Murphy, OCarm., Carmel Catholic High School, Mundelein, IL, used by permission)

## 1960–1969

*Nathan Coulter.* Boston: Houghton Mifflin, 1960 (revised North Point, 1985). Novel.

*The Broken Ground.* New York: Harcourt Brace, 1964. Poems.

*November twenty six nineteen hundred sixty three.* New York: Braziller, 1964. Poem.

*A Place on Earth.* Boston: Harcourt Brace, 1967 (revised North Point, 1983; Counterpoint, 2001). Novel.

*Findings.* Iowa City, IA: Prairie, 1968. Poems.

*Openings.* New York: Harcourt Brace, 1968. Poems.

*The Rise.* Lexington, KY: Grave, 1968. Essays.

*The Long-Legged House.* New York: Harcourt Brace, 1969 (Shoemaker & Hoard, 2004). Essays.

## 1970–1979

*Farming: A Hand Book.* New York: Harcourt Brace Jovanovich, 1970. Poems.

*The Hidden Wound.* Boston: Houghton Mifflin, 1970. Essays.

11

*The Unforeseen Wilderness: Kentucky's Red River Gorge.* Photographs by Ralph Eugene Meatyard. Lexington: University Press of Kentucky, 1971 (revised North Point, 1991; reissued and revised Shoemaker & Hoard, 2006). Essay.

*A Continuous Harmony: Essays Cultural and Agricultural.* New York: Harcourt Brace, 1972 (Shoemaker & Hoard, 2004). Essays.

*The Country of Marriage.* New York: Harcourt Brace Jovanovich, 1973. Poems.

*An Eastward Look.* Berkeley, CA: Sand Dollar, 1974. Poem.

*Horses.* Monterey, KY: Larkspur, 1974. Poem.

*The Memory of Old Jack.* New York: Harcourt Brace Jovanovich, 1974. (revised Counterpoint, 2001). Novel

*Sayings and Doings.* Lexington, KY: Gnomon, 1975. Poems.

*To What Listens.* Crete, NE: Best Cellar, 1975. Poem.

*The Kentucky River.* Monterey, KY: Larkspur, 1976. Poem.

*There Is Singing Around Me.* Austin: Cold Mountain, 1976. Poems.

*Clearing.* New York: Harcourt Brace Jovanovich, 1977. Poems.

*Three Memorial Poems.* Berkeley, CA: Sand Dollar, 1977. Poems.

*The Unsettling of America: Culture and Agriculture.* San Francisco: Sierra Club, 1977; Avon Books, 1978; Sierra Club, 1986. Essays.

## 1980–1989

*A Part.* San Francisco: North Point, 1980. Poems.

*The Gift of Good Land: Further Essays Cultural and Agricultural.* San Francisco: North Point, 1981. Essays.

*Recollected Essays, 1965–1980.* San Francisco: North Point, 1981. Essays.

*The Wheel.* San Francisco, North Point, 1982. Poems.

*Standing by Words.* San Francisco: North Point, 1983 (Shoemaker & Hoard, 2005). Essays.

*The Collected Poems, 1957–1982.* San Francisco: North Point, 1985. Poems.

*The Wild Birds: Six Stories of the Port William Membership.* San Francisco: North Point, 1986. Short stories.

*Home Economics: Fourteen Essays.* San Francisco: North Point, 1987. Essays.

*Sabbaths: Poems.* San Francisco: North Point, 1987. Poems.

*Remembering.* San Francisco: North Point, 1988. Novel.

*Traveling at Home.* San Francisco: Press Alley, 1988; North Point, 1989. Poems.

## 1990–1999

*Harlan Hubbard: Life and Work.* Lexington: University Press of Kentucky, 1990. Essay.

*What Are People For?* New York: North Point, 1990. Essays.

"The Discovery of Kentucky." Frankfort, KY: Gnomon, 1991. Short story.

*Fidelity.* New York: Pantheon, 1992. Short stories.

*Sex, Economy, Freedom, & Community.* New York: Pantheon, 1992. Essays.

"A Consent." Monterey, KY: Larkspur, 1993. Story.

*Watch with Me and Six Other Stories of the Yet-Remembered Ptolemy Proudfoot and His Wife, Miss Minnie, Née Quinch.* New York: Pantheon, 1994. Stories.

*Entries.* New York: Pantheon, 1994 (reprint Washington, DC: Counterpoint, 1997). Poems.

*The Farm.* Monterey, KY: Larkspur, 1995. Poem.

*Another Turn of the Crank.* Washington, DC: Counterpoint, 1996. Essays.

*A World Lost.* Washington, DC: Counterpoint, 1996. Novel.

*Two More Stories of the Port William Membership.* Frankfort, KY: Gnomon, 1997. Short stories.

*A Timbered Choir: The Sabbath Poems, 1979–1997.* Washington, DC: Counterpoint, 1998. Poems.

*The Selected Poems of Wendell Berry.* Washington, DC: Counterpoint, 1999. Poems.

## 2000–

*Jayber Crow.* Washington, DC: Counterpoint, 2000. Novel.

*Life Is a Miracle.* Washington, DC: Counterpoint, 2000. Essay.

*In the Presence of Fear: Three Essays for a Changed World*. Barrington, MA: Orion, 2001. Essays.

*Sonata at Payne Hollow*. Monterey, KY: Larkspur, 2001. Play.

*The Art of the Commonplace: The Agrarian Essays of Wendell Berry*. Ed. Norman Wirzba. Washington, DC: Counterpoint, 2002. Essays.

*Three Short Novels* [*Nathan Coulter, Remembering, A World Lost*]. Washington, DC: Counterpoint, 2002. Novels.

*Citizenship Papers*. Washington, DC: Shoemaker & Hoard, 2003. Essays.

*That Distant Land: The Collected Stories*. Washington, DC: Shoemaker & Hoard, 2004.

*Tobacco Harvest: An Elegy*. Photographs by James Baker Hall. Lexington: University Press of Kentucky, 2004. Essay.

*Hannah Coulter*. Washington, DC: Shoemaker & Hoard. 2004. Novel.

*Sabbaths 2002*. Monterey, KY: Larkspur, 2004. Poems.

*Blessed Are the Peacemakers: Christ's Teachings about Love, Compassion, and Forgiveness*. Washington, DC: Shoemaker & Hoard, 2005. A gathering, an introduction, and an essay.

*Given: New Poems*. Washington, DC: Shoemaker & Hoard, 2005. Poems.

*The Way of Ignorance and Other Essays*. Washington, DC: Shoemaker & Hoard, 2005. Essays.

*Andy Catlett: Early Travels*. Washington, DC: Shoemaker & Hoard, 2006. Novel.

# 1
. . . . . . . . . . . .
## A Necessary Voice

Imagine, if you will, an elderly rural man, past seventy but strong and stubborn, plowing a hillside behind a team of horses. At home, he scribbles away in a notebook, careful in his relationship to technology and fame. He is a family man, living within miles of his children—also farmers—and grandchildren, within miles of his birthplace. And the place he has chosen to live in north-central Kentucky, let alone being far from either the East or West Coast, is far from any of the centers of trade and technological development that have sprouted up around the nation. The railroad tracks and river that run through Henry County, Kentucky, hark back to a slower time, a lost time, a place not yet reinvented as a quaint Americana tourist haven or a neon-casino stopover. By every measure of our culture's urbanized (and suburbanized), high-tech, interconnected, media-savvy, consumeristic ethos, this man—Wendell Berry—would seem as irrelevant as a person could possibly be. But it would be a mistake to quickly label him a "redneck," since he sharply resists the privileging of urban sensibilities over rural. And he knows the difference. He has been a cosmopolitan man, a novelist living in Europe and New York, an academician at venerable universities. The fact that he now answers to the title "farmer" is a choice, thoughtfully cultivated and intentional.

Wendell Berry, whose vision we want to unpack over the course of these chapters, repudiated any standard definition of relevance long ago. He has become the fox of his own verse: "As soon as the generals and politicos / can predict the motions of your mind, / lose it. Leave it as a sign / to mark the false trail, the way / you didn't go. Be like the fox / who makes more tracks than necessary, / some in the wrong direction."[1]

Our immediate concern is whether such a figure, and the life he champions and lives, is more than simply a nostalgic call to a lost past, now superseded in almost every sphere of life.[2] What might compel us to listen to him amidst the cacophony of voices shouting at us from all directions? What would our society gain, and perhaps lose, by listening to him? What would the church in America learn if it could tune its ear to his persistent message? The last of these questions has a double edge, because Berry also owns up unequivocally to our dependence on the Creator God, our humility before God and in creation. His dogged irrelevance on the one hand unfolds into a dogged hope on the other, for his crafty "track-making" has the most deliberate of directions, as the final line of the poem quoted above reveals: "Practice resurrection."[3]

If we hear this call to "practice resurrection" in anything like a triumphalistic, or perhaps sentimental, tone—a mere substituting of the past for the present—then we need to retune to Berry's broader message. The allusive, poetic sense of it is not easily theologically reducible, but we do want to think about the implications of his life-giving vision, both in and around our Christian confessions. It is imperative that we recognize where our energies and efforts toward

---

1. "Manifesto: The Mad Farmer Liberation Front," in SP, 88.

2. Berry himself has recently declared that "history provides many examples of coherent communities, but not one that we can 'go back to.' We have no place to begin but where we are" ("The Purpose of a Coherent Community," in WI, 78). We are indebted to our student and friend Chris Allers for bringing this and several other important Berry quotes to our attention.

3. SP, 88.

"practicing resurrection," and realizing God's Kingdom in tangible ways, are limited; hence we must think long and hard about how and where to point our efforts.

So you can begin to see why, if we were asked to name one person to whom contemporary Christians need to listen, it would be this unlikely source, a man with no important connections to ecclesial or political or corporate power. In fact, it is Berry's abdication of power, his suspicion of all power that does not submit to limits of nature and personhood, that makes him so compelling. He declares no new good but reiterates the old, enduring good—he tells again and again the story of the way things should be, from an instructive past to a meaningful possible future in the midst of a forlorn present.

What does Berry help us to see? Well, probably we all recognize that something's wrong with globalized American culture, something about the restless, stressed, tremendously active, but often aimless modes by which we live. We are all further afflicted with that peculiar augment to this lifestyle, the constant stream of how-to manuals for more efficient living, for maximizing and capitalizing on life's opportunities. Under the illusion of getting somewhere, we are consumed by the effort to figure why we aren't there yet. And so our common life is often defined by failure: How many of us are untouched by divorce? How many of us haven't felt the dislocation of moving far from family? How many of us have not wondered aloud about the long-term effects of anonymous suburban sprawl reaching farther and farther into the countryside? The content of our life has become strangely defined by what we lack, by what is broken.

The two of us feel this estrangement acutely. Like most other Americans, we now live hundreds of miles from our birthplaces, the towns we grew up in, our "ancestral lands"—we feel the displacement every time our parents want to see their grandkids. We have each lived in several states (and Matt has even ranged north to Toronto) seeking the educational credentials to do what we do. We have each sought to put down deep roots in local church communities and to make ourselves more than just wayfarers in our local neighborhoods. These efforts have not been without success, nor

(margin note: from Gk, "ekklesiastikos," meaning "an assembly of citizens") has our effort to lead ourselves, our colleagues, and our students to think about becoming "at home." Berry has helped us not only in diagnosing the nature and range of the problems we face but in constructing ways of living that answer the call of faithfulness. Here is some of the fruit we have seen in our lives as we've worked under the umbrella of Berry's ideas: Matt serves on the planning commission of his rural township (whose motto is rather pointed: "To somehow embrace the growth we cannot stop and preserve some of the past we love so much") but also is committed with his family to the work of a century-old church that has tried to adjust to its role as an inner-city presence. Michael and his wife have helped revive the block-party tradition in their city neighborhood, using their front yard as a meeting place for neighbors who had never met one another over the years. Michael's family has also spent a decade at a small church on the fringe of Grand Rapids that is trying to make an impact on the apartment complexes next door (no surprise that the pastor is also an avid reader of Berry).

What's important to point out here is that we've not read Berry as a call to forsake technology and to join up in rural communes. He is never so simplistic. His call is much more about specific people in specific places building specific life-giving habits, a call stressing an integrity between the values we confess and the lives we embody. That's what we've tried to do with his ideas, to live them in small ways.

Thus, not only by standards of a creational order and a God who calls us to life but also by standards of coherent living in the here and now, Berry is stunningly relevant. In fact, he is necessary. The reasons why might not be immediately evident in any single essay or poem or story, but these reasons accrue as one reads through forty years' worth of writing, most of it against the cultural current. In his corpus of quiet, reflective fiction, in poems that range from invective to Sabbath prayers, and in essays that work in and around the demise of farming and local communities, he shows us again and again the devastation wrought by modernity. But these laments are always laced with possibilities for hope. His persistent question must become ours: how can we sustain meaningful lives against the background of a consumeristic, dislocated age?

The place of flourishing toward which Berry points seems counterintuitive: structural limits, kept through humility, burgeoning into hospitality, always vulnerable. Such limitation makes us aware of the gravity of our cultural disease but also reveals space for hope. Indeed, hope begins only in the acceptance of limit, as we shall see as we follow Berry's lead in tracing various crises—familial, economic, political—in order to understand the "lay of the land" of his critiques. Probably no other author in contemporary American public discourse has gained such currency in *both* progressive and conservative circles. Berry's dogged concern with place and community manages to connect those who are chiefly anxious about ecological crises and corporatization with those whose vested interests are in the preservation of tradition and rootedness. What makes Berry's ideas attractive to such a wide range of ideologies within our culture? Can the answers to our abstract global problems come through a reevaluation of our basic relationships, with particular people in particular places? What does it mean to assess the diseases of the church in America, and to trace the possible paths of healing, along the lines of Berry's thinking? How might the educational systems in our culture be chastened and relocated along the lines that Berry has hinted at? Though he doesn't offer a panacea for every woe, Berry does provide a way of answering "from somewhere," with a spirit and an approach of humility, wrestling with both the goodness and the fallenness of creation.

## A Patchwork Quilt

We see Berry's ideas as an old quilt, pleasing to the senses and also still surprisingly useful. The pieces have accumulated over the years, from many places, but he always works within a pattern. Let's get some of the basic contours. Berry was born in Henry County, Kentucky, in 1934, his father a lawyer but his grandparents and many friends Depression-era farmers. He witnessed the transformation to a tractor-based farm economy during and after World War II, and by the time he went off to a military boarding school for his high school education, the transition from "old school farming" to "new school farming," buoyed up by all the promises of mechanization, had taken hold. For Berry, the University of Kentucky, where he received his BA in 1956 and his MA in 1957, opened a path toward a literary career, and he began to write about Henry County from a distance. After marrying Tanya Amyx, daughter of an art history professor at Lexington, he studied at Stanford with the novelist Wallace Stegner, a formative figure for writing about rural roots. He lived in Italy and then lived and taught in New York at New York University. His journey at this time was really the journey that many Americans were taking, toward the East or West Coast, toward urban America, away from the heartland. But by the time he had written his first novel, *Nathan Coulter*, and first few books of poems, he had decided to make his way back to the University of Kentucky, a local boy made good.

Then, around age thirty, Berry returned to the farm, first for weekend retreats but soon as a whole-hearted investment of his life. What happened? In his essay "A Native Hill," written in the late 1960s, he recognizes that his cosmopolitan journey had been a preparation for something quite unexpected, something not wholly definable: "After more than thirty years I have at last arrived at the candor necessary to stand on this part of the earth that is so full of my own history and so much damaged by it, and ask: What *is* this place? What is in it? What is its nature? How should men live in it? What must I do?"[4]

4. ACP, 22. Here, we notice an interesting parallel to the basic worldview questions announced by J. Richard Middleton and Brian Walsh in *The Transforming Vision* (Downers Grove, IL: InterVarsity Press, 1984) and also by James Sire in *Discipleship of the Mind* (Downers Grove, IL: InterVarsity Press, 1990): "Where are we? Who are we? What's the problem? What's the solution?" Such a parallel is furthered by the questions that Berry poses in his extended argument in *Life Is a Miracle*, where he suggests we ponder not only "Where are we?" and "Who are we?" but also "What is our condition?" "What are our abilities?" and "What appropriately may we do in our own interest *here*?" (14).

It is exactly these questions that the modern world fails to answer, and Berry's sense of that dissonance, which he felt even in realizing the "perfect life" for a literary and scholarly aspirant, would not let him rest. These questions seem to have aroused in him a real need to understand *place* and *home* in some way far beyond a house and a geographic location. He was moved to look for the most basic motivations for why we are who we are and why we do what we do. The critical juncture was not the first phase, when Berry and his family visited the farm on weekends as a sort of retreat and a restoration project. Rather, it was the more extreme decision to actually live there, to dwell "in the farm" rather than just "on" or "at" it, that opened up the possibilities for thinking afresh about what humans are called to. It was his act of commitment, his act of "troth," his "fidelity," that made the flourishing possible, both for the farm and for his imagination. It then followed that Berry "quit" the university (his clarification to an interviewer who suggested that he had "retired")[5] as an institutional link that no longer corresponded to his vision—he had begun to feel "called out of" the typical institutions of American life.

The questions that Berry set before himself in his relocation to the land, though elusive, became answerable, at least in a limited way, because they were within the context of his commitment. Berry's addressing of the questions might best be described as *confessional*, in the sense that the answers have not been rationally calculated but affirmed by embodiment of a way of life. In the essay "A Native Hill," Berry posits the questions that led him to his land as those that ultimately lead him everywhere else: "They are part of the necessary enactment of humility, teaching a man what his importance is, what his responsibility is, and what his place is, both on the earth and in the order of things. And though the answers must always come obscurely and in fragments, the questions must be asked. They are fertile questions. In their implications and effects, they are moral and aesthetic and, in the best sense, practical. They promise

5. Thomas Healy, "A Conversation with Wendell Berry: Taking Care of What We've Been Given," *Counterpunch*, April 15–16, 2006.

*... re-establish our own connections to the land, to each other, and to [whatever it is we define as divine].*

a relationship to the world that is decent and preserving."[6] In the forty years since Berry returned with his wife and children back to Henry County and the Lane's Landing Farm, the fertility of these questions has been affirmed over and over in his writing. Coincidentally, the movement of late modernity, with its hyper-technological and hyper-consumptive habits, has brought his public reflection on these questions into startling contrast and relief. Any drive through southern Ohio and Indiana and through northern Kentucky reveals the inexorable creeping of suburbs outward, ring upon ring, a phenomenon long familiar along the East and West coasts (and even in a place like Grand Rapids, our staunchly Midwestern home). Likewise, the coming of Wal-Marts and strip malls and chain restaurants to Berry's neck of the woods can only have affirmed to him the urgent character of these essential questions.

Yet, from another angle, to the mere passerby Henry County and Port Royal in particular are part of the rural America "left behind" by the movements of modernity all around. Indeed, driving through rural Henry County looked to us a lot like driving through rural southeastern Ohio (Matt's roots), or rural upstate New York (Michael's roots), or rural central Michigan (the roots of many of our students), places tacitly determined by hyper-modernity as simply somewhere to be *from*.

Though Berry's move back home presaged the widespread "back to the land" movements of the early 1970s, his was not a romanticized endeavor. In the end, his move was a rediscovery, a way back home. For most of us, this seems fanciful because we have no ancestral land, no link back through three or four (or more) generations, no fallow farm waiting to be revivified and tended. But the power of Berry's rediscovery is the suggestion that we can be satisfied only when we have reestablished our own connections to the land, to one another, and to God. The fact that those three relationships are tightly interwoven for Berry is a crucial lesson we can learn alongside him. Likewise, we can recognize that the

6. ACP, 22.

duration of the project of reconnection, as Berry experiences and expresses it, is a lifetime. ✳ Yes..

After his move "back home," several concerns began to surface in Berry's essays and speeches, and especially the fiction, a set of realizations about the unsustainability of our culture's casual relationship to the land, the community, even the past. In his novels *Nathan Coulter*, published in 1960, and *A Place on Earth*, first published in 1967 and revised in the early 1980s, Berry began to wrestle through the history of Port William, his fictional universe based on the Port Royal of his childhood memories. The set of stories creates the place, and the place creates the stories, the people and their bonds to one another.[7]

Berry's work in the 1970s includes some of his richest poetry, as he celebrates the basic elements of the local community: marriage, household, and place. In his essays he is mainly lamenting and critiquing the demise of the farm economy, though in a few places, notably "Discipline and Hope"[8] and certainly in the seminal essay "The Body and the Earth,"[9] Berry's cultural observations begin to take shape as more than just social criticism. These lengthy reflections are among the places where we have sensed the coming together of a coherent vision for life, of which this book is our attempt at an exposition. These are important moments in his development, though most of the essay collections are patchworks of the best sort, observations rooted in particulars of either his own experience in farming or of others he has taken the time to know, pieces written "along the way" by an active farmer.[10] In the late 1980s and through the 1990s,

---

7. One of Berry's clear literary models for such world-making is William Faulkner with his elaborate vision of Yoknawpatawpha County, Mississippi, the fictional world that he builds out of his own people and place but that grows into a world of its own.

8. From the 1972 collection *A Continuous Harmony*.

9. From the 1977 collection *The Unsettling of America*.

10. The actual prompting for many of the essays has been incidental and situational, though the collections are by no means random assortments of ideas. Many essays stem from visits to various farms (both in his neighborhood and, sometimes, in other countries). The pattern that emerges is a constant return to the basic principles of care, limit, humility—though the situations where this formula is applied vary greatly, such as in "Irish Journal" (1982), "An Agricultural Journey in Peru" (1979), and "Elmer Lapp's Place" (1979).

Berry's essays began to reach a growing subculture through journals like *Orion, Mother Jones,* and *Organic Gardening.* Here, the connections between the struggles of family farms and small towns and the rising industrial and technological complex of contemporary society become more conspicuous. Although his concerns are often environmental, they are never purely such—the crisis in the environment is always seen as a part of a broader demise of human concerns. His critiques of the academy are likewise not part of the discourse inside of higher education so much as criticisms of the academy's allegiance to the corporate economic systems.

Having spoken to the grave crises of his own milieu, and having put forward a dogged vision for life throughout forty years of stories, poems, and essays, Berry was in a unique position, in the wake of the September 11, 2001, terrorist attacks, to offer a substantial response. When brought to bear on that tragic moment, all the weight of his ongoing critique, as well as all the fragile hope that he had built, was put to the test. His critique became explicitly a critique of empire, of an entire societal vision at odds with life and health. Though social critics were agreed that the 9/11 attacks signaled a new shape to the world, this new shape was no surprise to Berry—he had been lamenting the forces bending the world toward such a cataclysm for his whole career. At its root his work had always decried the constant state of war brought about by an inability, or unwillingness, to prepare for peace, economically, socially, or otherwise.

Hence with the publication of *In the Presence of Fear: Three Essays for a Changed World* in 2001, Berry's consistent ideas became somewhat famous and rather controversial.[11] Certainly, to comment on national security strategies and international affairs has opened up Berry to far more censure than did his considerations of the farming life—though if he is out of his comfort zone, his concern is still ultimately for the health of local communities everywhere, however clearly or obscurely this might translate into national policy. What

11. See especially the special edition of the *South Atlantic Quarterly* (101, no. 2, Spring 2002), guest edited by Stanley Hauerwas and Frank Lentricchia, titled "Dissent from the Homeland: Essays after September 11."

made Berry's critique stick, and what gave strength to the subsequent volumes *Citizenship Papers* and *The Way of Ignorance*, was that despite the bristly tone of many of the pieces, they fit into a broader, deeper mosaic that has always been rooted in a hopefulness for life, a belief that care is a viable alternative to exploitation, that the social soil can be rebuilt even when it's been stripped to the stone. Berry said as far back as 1970, in the first chapter of *The Hidden Wound*, his rumination on the legacy of slavery and racism, that he wanted to tell the ugly truth because of "an obligation to make the attempt, and I know if I fail to make at least the attempt I forfeit any right to hope the world will become better than it is now."[12]

Berry's evolving vision for life cannot be articulated from any single work or even through any single genre—it has grown, as he has observed often of the growing of forests as "hardwood crops," over the course of decades, thoughtfully tended but not overtended. What he said of Irish agriculture in 1982 could likely also be said of his own writing: "Thus, coming to Ireland has reminded me again how long, complex, and deep must be the origins of the best work of any kind."[13]

## Health in the Midst of Disease

If we had to boil down a whole career of lively and varied discourse into a single theme, it would be Berry's dogged search for health in the midst of disease. His notion of health is undergirded by a set of ideas that includes finitude, humility, localness, boundedness, propriety of scale, particularity. Obviously these are not the buzzwords of our current cultural discourse, most of which would pull in the opposite direction: global, comprehensive, progressive, efficient, profitable. But Berry's analysis reveals that this second list harbors phrases that are often masks, ideas that seem polished and powerful on the surface yet refuse to give an account of full humanness, and so hide profound disease.

12. HW, 4.
13. HE, 45.

One of the texts that makes visible this fundamental tension of health versus disease is "Health is Membership," originally a talk given at a conference on "Spirituality and Healing" in 1994. What is striking in Berry's account of health and wholeness here, as elsewhere, is its communal nature: "If we were lucky enough as children to be surrounded by grown-ups who loved us, then our sense of wholeness is not just the sense of completeness in ourselves but also is the sense of belonging to others and to our place; it is an unconscious awareness of community. It may be that this double sense of singular integrity and of communal belonging is our personal standard of health for as long as we live. Anyhow, we seem to know instinctively that health is not divided."[14] The creational root of such an understanding of health is made explicit by Berry later in the essay, when he asserts, "I take literally the statement in the Gospel of John that God loves the world. . . . I believe that divine love, incarnate and indwelling in the world, summons the world always toward wholeness, which ultimately is reconciliation and atonement with God."[15] Hence Berry understands health as wholeness in and between humans, toward creation, and before God; this health requires accepting the boundaries of creational existence, revealed in both creation and incarnation. And as the follower of Christ is only intelligible as such in the context of the larger body of Christ, so a healthy person is such only by reference to the community: "I believe that the community—in the fullest sense: a place and all its creatures—is the smallest unit of health and that to speak of the health of an isolated individual is a contradiction in terms."[16]

Another place where Berry articulates his vision of health and healing is his essay "Two Minds." Here his language becomes explicitly confessional, rooted firmly in the notion that our basic direction in life flows from the commitments of the heart. Berry notes that "most of the most important laws for the conduct of human life probably are religious in origin—laws such as these: Be merciful, be forgiving,

14. ACP, 144–45.
15. Ibid., 146.
16. Ibid.

love your neighbors, be hospitable to strangers, be kind to other creatures, take care of the helpless, love your enemies. We must, in short, love and care for one another and the other creatures. We are allowed to make no exceptions. Every person's obligation toward the Creation is summed up in two words from Genesis 2:15: 'Keep it.'"[17] The inability to see things as they truly are always leads to a "selfishness, or even 'enlightened self-interest,' [that] cannot find a place to poke in its awl. One's obligation to oneself cannot be isolated from one's obligation to everything else. The whole thing is balanced on the verb *to love*."[18] Wholeness, health, love—a set of notions emerges toward which we must bend our efforts within the flow of community. Only in dedication to the human face in each exchange can we enact a healthful love.

Berry identifies the "Sympathetic Mind" as "the mind of our creatureliness,"[19] as well as "the mind of our wholeness"[20] and "a preeminently faithful mind, taking knowingly and willingly the risks required by faith."[21] In opposition is the prideful blindness of the "Rational Mind," which "is objective, analytical, and empirical; it makes itself up only by considering facts; it pursues truth by experimentation; it is uncorrupted by preconception, received authority, religious belief, or feeling."[22] Not surprisingly, Berry lodges this view as "the official mind of science, industry, and government."[23] This mind knows by reducing and fragmenting, ultimately breaking apart relationships for the sake of comprehension and mastery. This is yet another mask of deception, where disease has the cultural label of health.

But the "Sympathetic Mind" is cognizant of finitude as a part of interdependence. It "accepts loss and suffering as the price, willingly

17. CZP, 103.
18. Ibid.
19. Ibid., 91.
20. Ibid., 92.
21. Ibid., 93.
22. Ibid., 88.
23. Ibid.

paid, of its sympathy and affection—its wholeness."[24] Furthermore, it "accepts life in this world for what it is: mortal, partial, fallible, complexly dependent, entailing many responsibilities toward ourselves, our places, and our fellow beings. Above all it understands itself as limited."[25]

This summoning toward wholeness, with the recognition of partiality and fallibility, demands that we think of health not as arrival but rather as aspiration, as eschatological promise. This path to health that Berry supports is not utopian[26] nor infinite in possibilities; even in the midst of disease one can still discern the way. Health thus doesn't demand or produce eternal life but rather a reconciliation with creation as it now stands. Health is dynamic, an infinite call to heal.

Berry's vision is not a new metaphysic—another world offered as an escape from fallenness and despair. Instead, the story to be told is one of healing within the bounds of creation, not yet a final resurrection, not yet a new creation. Nowhere does Berry articulate this more eloquently than in the long essay "The Body and the Earth." Here the mask is seen as the glossy embodiment of human pride, a pride that reduces the world to its mechanical functions: "We become less and less capable of sensing ourselves as small within Creation . . . because we were becoming creators, ourselves, of a mechanical creation by which we felt ourselves greatly magnified."[27] But Berry also elaborates on the theme of blessed limitation which characterizes the "Sympathetic Mind." When we perceive that "healing is impossible in loneliness; it is the opposite of loneliness,"[28] we are back at the root of healing, the communal recognition and obligation. This

---

24. Ibid., 92.

25. Ibid., 100.

26. Though Berry is no escapist or sociopolitical hyper-idealist, there is a strong vision in his work of future hope informing present practice. He set out early in his writings this notion of a guiding ideal, "our only guide to the future" though it is "apparent and meaningful [only] in relation to the real" ("The Loss of the Future," in LLH, 48). Elsewhere in this book we appeal to the notion of eschatological hope to capture Berry's ideal, but this hope is always colored by our fallenness and our seeing "through a glass darkly."

27. ACP, 96.

28. Ibid., 98.

extends outward, not with the universalizing or totalizing motive of modernity, for such a motive would reject the very particularity that makes community possible. But there is a sweeping scope to this healing: "to be healed, we must come with all the other creatures to the feast of Creation."[29] We explore many of the embodiments of this healing in later chapters, but here we want to call attention to the shape of the vision.

To be explicit, we understand this vision to be a worldview[30]—this creates our interpretive framework, whereby we can say that Berry offers a vision for life—and even if readers disagree with particular policies and outworkings of it, the root vision is world-revealing, alive, and life-giving. We understand worldviews to be confessional, to be pretheoretical orientations to reality, so our earlier mention of the confessional nature of Berry's work (both physical and intellectual) also points to the worldview connection.

In Berry's work we distinguish the contours of the Reformational worldview, articulated in the goodness of creation, the disease of fallenness, and the promise of redemption. On this third point, the redemptive hope, we would, however, offer a few words of clarification. Berry has rarely cast his work in terms formally theological or philosophical, and so it is tenuous to hold him to systematized categories. Nevertheless, his vision promotes a dynamic understanding of created reality, where the promised future can be made present. To say that Berry has an eschatological hope, as we do repeatedly in this book, is not to place upon his vision any overlay of theological precision—we're not talking about the pre/a/post-millennial divides, nor the purely future Kingdom, but rather an organic understanding that what we do in and with creation right now, through the constraints of fallenness, has continuity with the Kingdom's reality.

So if the end in mind for Berry is healing, how must we adjust our lives in the here and now? First is the recognition of finitude, a limitedness that is bound up in particularity of place and community

29. Ibid.
30. We'll explore this term further in chapter 4, especially its imaginative rather than rational nuances.

and interdependence in creation. This is a countercultural notion in every sense; there is no path toward healing in modern culture—economic or political or religious—that does not lead back to the difficult labor of recognizing and honoring our finitude. The structure of creation requires this. We cannot treat the ground beneath our feet, the bodies we dwell in, and the communities that shape us as indifferent nodes.

Alongside these structural limits, there is a spiritual necessity of humility that can grow into hospitality. This is a stance of vulnerability—not of self-defense—since we can easily be displaced and trespassed upon. Yet healing cannot occur in a posture of self-protection, of impermeable boundaries. The challenge is world-shaping, radical, magnificently risky—and ultimately resonant with the call of the gospel.

## The Pattern of the Quilt

For such claims to have purchase, we need to do a thoroughgoing, careful reading of Berry's patchwork vision, allowing his voice to speak through the pages. Here is the path we've laid out.

In chapter 2, we will point out the enormously diverse range of social critics who have found Berry's ideas useful; the point here will be to ponder how and why he has captured the imaginations of people across the ideological spectrum. Conservatives, liberals, libertarians, secularists, agrarians, new urbanists—Berry has managed, in his thorny way, to capture at least a portion of the imagination of each of these diverse groups. The fact of his wide attraction offers more than a hint at the compelling urgency of his message.

In chapter 3, we will read Berry's essential paradox of health versus disease at a few different levels, as a way to show its richness and resilience as his basic trope with which to understand our culture. We'll look at the "intellectual order" as the place where different social visions are hashed out, different spiritual orientations toward the world. Next, we'll discuss the outworking of these ideas in time and place as the "social order," with sharp contrasts made between the

Kingdom of God at work in shaping the world and a radical utilitarianism which seeks its own reshaping. We'll finish by contrasting the level of the "personal human order," where different understandings of a fully realized individual will be weighed. Whether in terms of spiritual vision, social ordering, or personal satisfactions, the root cause of disease is shown in the dislocation from particular people in particular places. And out of this unified critique, we see Berry pointing toward a coherent vision for healing.

Chapter 4 will be our most philosophical, as we seek to understand Berry's account of limits through a differentiation of structure and direction. Here we will hazard a more theoretical examination of Berry's understanding of creation and of the fall. Our desire is not to superimpose on Berry's ideas but rather to defend him from certain misreadings. To those who want to see him as a nostalgist, an oversimplifier, an agrarian crank, or a snob, we seek to show that a more systematic approach can be taken to his ideas than his mode of delivery might suggest. We want to extend the range of those with whom his ideas might foster conversation, not just to make peace with his detractors (we're not sure he'd want that!) but because the ideas are worthy of such engagement.

Chapter 5 begins our account of the paths of healing and relocation that Berry offers, starting from the ground up with his account of our relationship to the soil, earth, and food. Chapter 6 will then extend this account through his anticipatory categories where healing must occur: body, marriage, household, and finally local community. This isn't a prescriptive formula but rather a fragile, hopeful vision, threatened always by the pervasive possibility of disembodiment and abstraction.

In chapter 7, we'll continue to follow Berry along the lines of tension between health and disease, by showing the boundaries both of individualism and of globalism, anchoring in both instances on the need for a local community to offer healthy identity. We'll trace some of the trespasses of wrong-minded individualism and of wrong-minded globalization, in an effort to reveal the bad thinking at the root of both.

Chapter 8 will be a conversation about the way these boundaries need to work if we are to carry out the vision for hospitality that is at the center especially of Berry's fiction works. How can the boundaries of community be both firm and permeable? What role does the keeping and telling of stories play in protecting these boundaries? A survey of Berry's novels and stories shows the difficult balance necessary to make hospitality alive.

By chapter 9, we will have hopefully earned our right, by means of defining and unfolding Berry's vision, to extend this vision to the church, with the intention of offering a fresh and vitalizing way of understanding our kingdom tasks.

Finally, in chapter 10 we'll try to stretch our privilege yet further in order to bring to bear this healing vision to the realm of education and its practices, not only within the institutions of teaching but also in the extended teaching and learning "workshop" of political and economic life. This is the place where Berry's voice has carried prophetic weight for us. If by the end of the journey we have made enough space for Wendell Berry's full range of ideas to show through and have given a sort of guided tour of the ends and aims that evolve from them, then we will have done our labor well.

# 2

## Wendell Berry's Creational Vision

As we unfold the breadth of Berry's vision and the wide range of thinkers who have been drawn to it, we should begin by saying that it is attractive and relevant in no small measure because he speaks bluntly to the deep troubles of our age. The problems of our culture—disease, dislocation, outrageous hubris—are so massive that they present a formidable roadblock to any substantive discourse about true health. The broader context of our lives is a violence and meaninglessness that permeated the twentieth century and bleeds into the twenty-first. We live within a darkness that the theologian Walter Lowe has lamented as "the shadow of mass violence cast by . . . the century of total war."[1] Since perhaps the beginning of World War I, the whole world has existed under either the threat or the direct influence of ever-advancing military technology and its economic and political ramifications. Even in such retrogressive regimes as the Taliban in Afghanistan, there is an impulse to participate in the global reach

1. Walter Lowe, *Theology and Difference: The Wound of Reason* (Bloomington: Indiana University Press, 1993), 1. Also, in an intriguing gloss, at the beginning of Berry's novel *Jayber Crow*, Jayber reflects that he "was born at Goforth, on Katy's Branch, on August 3, 1914—and so lived one day in the world before the beginning of total war" (11).

of destructive technologies. There is certainly no place untouchable, and few places as yet untouched, by the possibilities of violence and repression. The geopolitical situation of our time is characterized by both deliberate and random violence, whole populations of refugees, the enduring effects of modern empires, horrifying pandemics of AIDS and other diseases ravaging Africa and parts of Asia, and even the threats within our own democracy of plutocratic rule and reprisal.

Closer to home in every sense, we depend upon unsustainable production and delivery of foods from around the globe and across the continent, straight to our tables on demand. This is not only an issue of agricultural or economic concern: it also falls under the ubiquitous shadow of national security and global politics. When we first learned that a local juice company in western Michigan purchased its juice concentrate from China rather than working with the prodigious local apple orchards literally right down the road, we were rather stunned. Furthermore, the threats imposed on small towns dominated by single employers have been manifested locally: Greenville, Michigan appeared unexpectedly on BBC World News because the Electrolux factory pulled up its stakes and moved to Mexico, leaving an entire community reeling as a casualty of global economic margins. This sort of discontinuity has been played out over and over again in Michigan, and indeed in many parts of the world, as the mobility of corporations is mimicked by the mobility of those left to search for a new way to make a living. The Grand Rapids Public School System serves as an example of a different sort of abandonment, as suburban sprawl has drawn away resources and people, leaving urban school kids to struggle with shrinking resources and constant restructuring. Likely you could think of two or three parallel examples in your own region, so ubiquitous are the diseases that afflict our culture.

Over and over again, we encounter strategies for living that are at odds with life. But these threats, both real and potential, can either crush us under their weight or push us toward alternative ways of being in the world. The potential slide into meaninglessness can invite an overhaul, a "renarration," of our place or places within the world.

## Berry among the Truth-Tellers

We are not totally bereft of guides in this crisis, but the voices are scattered and require hard listening. They tend to offend the powers that be. Stanley Hauerwas, for one, has been helpful in pointing to a few sources of light. Toward the end of his set of Gifford Lectures, collected in the book *With the Grain of the Universe*, Hauerwas has a chapter called "The Necessity of Witness" in which he offers John Paul II, John Howard Yoder, and Wendell Berry as three crucial voices exhorting the church to a properly countercultural vision of life.[2] The first two names are no surprise to readers of Hauerwas, since they fit the first two parts of his polyglot theological moniker "Catholic-Mennonite-Southern Methodist." It is Berry who seems the surprising inclusion here. What has he to do with these towering theologians of our time? The short answer, at least for now, is that they have much in common: All three men have been critical of our contemporary loss of direction and of the church's complicity in this. Alongside Berry's lament of the loss of place one could easily posit John Paul II's lament of the loss of personhood and Yoder's lament of the loss of authenticity. Furthermore, all three seek to sketch a hopeful course of recovery; they function as lights that not only expose the works of darkness, but which help us to see forward. Of the three, Berry represents the fullest embodiment of telling "the Story" through stories (despite the young Karel Wojtyla's playwriting and poetry, he and Yoder will be remembered as theologians and not artists). Berry's work is precisely the sort of "renarration" that can bring healing and make visible the call to "practice resurrection," just as the other two have tried through their work to embody the calls to "cross the threshold of hope" and to "practice the politics of Jesus."

The juxtaposition to Yoder, the salient apologist for Christian pacifism in the late twentieth century and Hauerwas's mentor, underscores the fundamental commitment to peacemaking that Berry

---

2. *With the Grain of the Universe: The Church's Witness and Natural Theology* (Grand Rapids: Brazos, 2001), 232–33.

has shown since his earliest published essays in condemnation of the Vietnam War. In a speech given at the University of Kentucky in 1968, "A Statement against the War in Vietnam," Berry very much resonates a Yoderian theme when he takes to task the notion that "if America were to become peaceable, and to live up to her Christian and democratic ideals, surely some warlike nation would destroy her. I do not know how to reply to that objection except to ask in return: Does the hope of peace lie in waiting for peace, or in being peaceable? If I see what is right, should I wait for the world to see it, or should I make myself right immediately, and thus be an example to the world?"[3] This notion of peace as more than opposition to violence but rather an active model for human growth and flourishing certainly exemplifies the foundational premises for a vision of life that Yoder and Hauerwas have boldly championed. In the 9/11-shadowed "Thoughts in the Presence of Fear," Berry sharpens the point he made a generation earlier: "In a time such as this, when we have been seriously and most cruelly hurt by those who hate us, and when we must consider ourselves to be gravely threatened by those same people, it is hard to speak of the ways of peace and to remember that Christ enjoined us to love our enemies, but this is no less necessary for being difficult." Further, "what leads to peace is not violence but peaceableness, which is not passivity, but an alert, informed, practiced, and active state of being."[4] Yet, for all of his affinity with Yoder's radically Christocentric vision, a focused understanding of "the politics of Jesus" centered on peacemaking, Berry follows a branch of a more fundamental stem, a creation-centric vision that finds even stronger affinity in the connection to John Paul II.

The corollary of the late John Paul II is a useful, but also very daunting, aid in understand Berry's vision. In the encyclical *Evangelium Vitae*, John Paul II laid out the ethical terrain of our era by casting all human choice as leading toward either a "culture of life" or a "culture of death." These terms, much co-opted and at times diluted, have nevertheless retained a power of accuracy and simplicity.

3. LLH, 72–73.
4. CZP, 20.

In section 24 of the encyclical, John Paul II extends his critique of the debased individual "moral conscience" when he suggests that "it is also a question, in a certain sense, of the 'moral conscience' of society: in a way it too is responsible, not only because it tolerates or fosters behavior contrary to life, but also because it encourages the 'culture of death,' creating and consolidating actual 'structures of sin' which go against life."[5] Here we find the broadest possible scale upon which to weigh ourselves not only individually but also communally. Berry is thus a purveyor of the "culture of life" and a sharp critic of the "culture of death." Everywhere in his work, in the essays and the fiction and the poetry, by virtue of the agricultural rubric of growth and harvest, fattening and butchering, he is constantly trying to properly measure life and death, to see how they fit together rightly within what he unabashedly loves: God's creation.

But it is also important to contrast Berry to John Paul II in a way that will prove central to our articulation of Berry's vision. The late pope's concerns were often drawn to the radical poles of birth and death. John Paul II's virulent criticisms of both abortion and euthanasia, and indeed all of his labors to get humankind to recognize what is at stake in skewing definitions of what it means to be alive and what it means to die, carry a tacit critique of modernity. Dehumanization, the loss of the meaningfulness of personhood, was the root addressed by the philosophical personalism that so deeply influenced his thought from his student days in Krakow onward.

While John Paul II was expressly concerned with the issues of limit in human life and death,[6] Berry works more in the terrain in between. Embodied, daily life was not outside of John Paul II's concern—he wrote at length on living fully, aesthetically, vocationally—but he

5. *Evangelium Vitae* 24.
6. Berry explicitly criticizes abortion as a sign of radical autonomy in "Rugged Individualism" (WI, 10), and the long story "Fidelity" is an extended treatment of issues of death and dying, as Burley Coulter's family seeks to understand how to let a "good life" end with a "good death." In between, Berry has much to teach the body of Christ about what it means to be alive in this world, fully located, fully enmeshed in community, fully a part of creation. He approvingly quotes Robert Southey's encomium of Admiral Nelson regarding the elusive "life fully lived": "a formal completeness that had little to do with its extent, and much to do with its accomplishments" ("Quantity vs. Form," in WI, 83).

was decisively concerned with the beginning- and end-of-life issues. Berry has used the pope's terms in his essay "Agriculture from the Roots Up," when he echoes questions posed at his friend Wes Jackson's Land Institute of Kansas, which extend from land to culture to people: "The answers, as these scientists know, will reveal not only the state of health of the landscape, but also the state of the culture of the people who inhabit and use the landscape. Is it a culture of respect, thrift, and seemly skills, or a culture of indifference and mechanical force? A culture of life or a culture of death?"[7] Berry seems to be looking at the full spectrum of influences that point toward either life or death, and for this he finds fruitful the polarity of health versus disease.[8] Since modernity dehumanizes not only at the poles of life but also at every point along the journey, we find ourselves distancing humanity from everything, even our selves. The land on which we live, walk, and sleep, the neighbors whose lives are lived a few feet from ours and yet too often light-years away, the ephemeral work of our hands that we so rarely can admire and contemplate—all of these disjunctures are faced daily and hourly. To discover the elusive "life fully lived," Berry suggests, is to answer these questions adequately: why we are here, who we are, and what we may appropriately do in our own interests here. Only then can we begin to overcome the distances, and to make the connections that he identifies as "health."

## Conservative Postmodern / Postmodern Conservative?

Building from such connections, we would like to show an even broader range of influence, as Berry proves a surprising nexus for many seemingly diverse interests. Indeed, his ideas are surprisingly applicable and attractive across a wide ideological spectrum. The root vision that he espouses has an amazing range—a vision that can bring into a common conversation such far-flung camps as classical

7. WI, 109.

8. Berry gets close to John Paul II's parlance in his essay "Quantity vs. Form," where he speaks of "the wheel of death" (WI, 86).

conservatives (e.g., Russell Kirk) and postmodern theorists (e.g., Jacques Derrida), such diverse Christian thinkers as Stanley Hauerwas, Eugene Peterson, and Brian Walsh, even the apologist for secular democracy Jeffrey Stout. This is not mere coincidence or rhetorical flourish. All of these people seem to be aware of the threats implicit in the modern world. In responding to these threats, Berry pushes the conversation back to basic concerns and direction-giving forces that appeal to this wide range of ideologies. He does not so much address each angle as enliven the conversation about "first things" that roots them all.

For the classic conservative (a different animal from the "right-wing" or "Republican" version of conservative in American parlance today—though not unrelated), it is surely Berry's defense of tradition, of stability over innovation, of devotion to the land and to the mores of the people on that land, that creates affinity. This shows in the work of Russell Kirk, the intellectual catalyst behind the resurgence of conservatism in American politics in the second half of the twentieth century. Kirk, like Berry, chose to live in his ancestral home, making his declarations from rural Mecosta, Michigan, rather than some endowed academic chair or Washington appointment. In 1953 he published *The Conservative Mind*, a tracing of ideas moored in Edmund Burke's critique of the French Revolution. Parallels to Berry's concerns are abundant in Kirk's articulation of this classic conservatism, and the language often anticipates Berry's themes of health versus morbidity. At the end of his introduction, "The Idea of Conservatism," Kirk asserts, "Burke, could he see our century, never would concede that a consumption-society, so near to suicide, is the end for which Providence has prepared men."[9] Likewise, in his final chapter, "The Recrudescence of Conservatism," much that Kirk outlines as the conservative critique and the conservative agenda resonates deeply with Berry's concerns, with a few crucial differences. Respect for the finitude and localness of human life can be found in Kirk's declaration that "Conservatism must teach

9. Russell Kirk, *The Conservative Mind: From Burke to Santayana* (Chicago: Regnery, 1953), 10.

humanity once more that the germ of public affections (in Burke's words) is 'to love the little platoon we belong to in society.' "[10] The task is also cast as the need to "redeem the modern masses from the sterile modern mass-mind."[11]

Kirk finds an interesting ally in perhaps the most famous socialist writer of the twentieth century, George Orwell, whose critique of the purveyors of the absolutist state "had been shaped and brought together by the barren world of monopoly industry and centralized government."[12] Kirk redirects the focus from the sociopolitical to the moral as he continues the description: "schooled beyond their proper worldly prospects or, indeed, beyond their intellectual capacities, lacking property, lacking religious faith, lacking ancestors or expectation of posterity, seeking to gratify by the acquisition of power their loneliness and their nameless hungers."[13] Furthermore, when Kirk lays out the four chief problems for conservatism to solve in the second half of the twentieth century, at least two of them are central to Berry's vision of life and health. The first Kirk casts as "the problem of spiritual and moral regeneration; the restoration of the ethical system and religious sanction upon which any life worth living is founded."[14] Berry's recognition of human life as a piece of creation, with the attendant reverence and humility, comes up close to Kirk's reflection. Another issue raised by Kirk, which he calls "the problem of the proletariat,"[15] doesn't sound at first like a Berryesque concern, but when Kirk sharpens his invective, the parallels are clear:

> The mass of men must find status and hope within society: true family, respect for private property, duty as well as right, inner resources that matter more than the mass-amusements and mass-vices with which the modern proletarian seeks to forget his lack of an object. . . . To

10. Ibid., 401.
11. Ibid.
12. Ibid., 409.
13. Ibid.
14. Ibid., 414.
15. Ibid., 415.

restore purpose to labor and domestic, to give men back old hopes and long views and thought of posterity, will require the bold imagination which Burke infused into conservative ideas.[16]

Here we see that Burke, rather than a more expected figure like Thomas Jefferson, is perhaps the most apt antecedent for Berry's agrarian vision.

More recent connections of Berry's vision have been made in the long-cast shadow of Kirk. In *The University Bookman*, a review founded by Kirk in the 1950s and now published by his widow, Annette Kirk, and edited by his son-in-law Jeffrey Nelson, included a review of books on New Agrarianism from 2002 that reveals this lasting connection.[17] The reviewer, Jeremy Beer, a senior editor at ISI Books, another place where Kirk's ideas are foundational, delves into two very different works, one academic and one populist. A common feature of Allan Carlson's *The New Agrarian Mind: The Movement toward Decentralist Thought in Twentieth-Century America* (from the intellectually right-leaning Transaction Publishers) and *The New Agrarianism: Land, Culture, and the Community of Life*, edited by Eric T. Freyfogle for the small environmentalist Island Press, is the figure of Wendell Berry. Carlson's assessment of the movement of New Agrarianism in general is rather mixed, and Beer points out that though the tenets of the movement have included "an abiding belief in the unique social importance of country living and the working family farm," an ironic twist is that "the agrarian proponents' seduction by modernity and secularization made the continued viability of the family farm impossible."[18] Beer notes, "Of course, some New Agrarian minds were more perceptive than others. Berry and [Andrew] Lytle, for instance, gain high praise from Carlson, though even they receive criticism."[19] Such praise of Berry is notable here, since it is clearly hard won.

16. Ibid.
17. Jeremy Beer, "Who Are the New Agrarians?" *The University Bookman* 42, no. 1 (2002): 28–31.
18. Ibid., 29.
19. Ibid.

The anthology edited by Freyfogle also features Berry prominently, and Beer emphasizes that the tacit conservatism of Berry and other like-minded New Agrarians, with its focus on "family and community health, and individual virtue as the fundamental issues at stake, not limitations of 'property rights,' viewed in the abstract," is in fact "perfectly in accord with the best of the conservative intellectual tradition."[20] Beer seems most impressed by the embodied nature of this sort of philosophy: "The writers Freyfogle has selected shape their lives in particular, concrete ways to be culturally conservative (though they may not label them as such). In contrast, political conservatives typically preach about the benefits of local control, community integrity, and cultural heterogeneity while pursuing lifestyles drastically at odds with such goals."[21] Berry, by this assessment, ends up more conservative, by virtue of his lived commitments, than many who actively espouse the title—a strong endorsement, and a chastening one as well for thinkers of the Right.

An analogue to this sort of conservatism, one embodied in healthy community and human virtue, is extolled in another journal article from 2002 in a publication with ties to Kirk, the *Intercollegiate Review*, published by the Intercollegiate Studies Institute. The fall 2002 issue includes an article by Peter Augustine Lawler titled "Conservative Postmodernism, Postmodern Conservatism." Lawler asserts, "Conservatives can be (perhaps the only) *genuinely* postmodern thinkers. The reason we can see beyond the modern world is that its intention to transform human nature has failed. Its project of transforming the human person into the autonomous individual was and remains unrealistic; we can now see the limits of being an individual because we remain more than individuals. The world created by modern individuals to make themselves fully at home turns out to have made human beings less at home than

20. Ibid., 31.
21. Ibid. See also Beer's excellent review of Berry's selected agrarian essays, edited by Norman Wirzba into the volume *The Art of the Commonplace* (in the equally Kirkian journal *Modern Age*, Summer 2003, 254–58). Beer is particularly acute here in placing Berry with the conservative strand.

ever."[22] This dislocation, lamented by Berry as a part of the "un-settling of America," has a corollary in the lack of purpose that Lawler sees in the modern individual who "has no particular view of what a free and comfortable human being should do with his comfort and freedom."[23] This ambiguity about basic principles of life and pleasure is a target of many of Berry's laments—he gives it an economic edge in the essay "What Are People For?" when he asks, "In a country that puts an absolute premium on labor-saving measures, short workdays, and retirement, why should there be any surprise at permanence of unemployment and welfare dependency? Those are only different names for our national ambitions."[24]

When Lawler finally epitomizes modernity's chief enemy as the specter of limitation, especially of natural death, he is surely drawing upon the notions of John Paul II (and explicitly upon St. Thomas), but he is also voicing a chief theme of Berry's work. Lawler might easily have included Berry in his comment that "it takes postmodern conservative outsiders like Aleksandr Solzhenitsyn (and Mother Teresa of Calcutta) to both notice and have the courage to say that Americans are more lonely and death-obsessed than ever before."[25] The reckoning with finitude, and death as the ultimate exclamation point upon our finitude, is a crucial function of community for Berry, who, especially in his fictional annals of Port William, Kentucky, echoes back Lawler's claim that "both love of each other and love of the truth depend, as far as we can tell, on the inevitability of death."[26] People die in Port William, but through stories they live on in the community, continuing to teach and delight. So Lawler's trope of the "conservative postmodernist" finds an interesting possible exemplar in Berry, whose work resounds with the humble aspiration that Lawler sees as his own central tenet: "The beginning of the postmodern world is the replacement of the individual by the whole

22. Peter Augustine Lawler, "Conservative Postmodernism, Postmodern Conservatism," *Intercollegiate Review* 38, no. 1 (Fall 2002): 17.
23. Ibid., 19.
24. WPF, 125.
25. Lawler, 23.
26. Ibid., 24.

human being, and the using of our natural capabilities for thought and action to make the world worthy of him."[27]

When it comes to actual postmodern theorists and philosophers, one might expect the sorts of connections posited by Lawler's redefinitions to be roundly rejected. However, affinities, both in the mutual critique of modernity and in the proximity to Berry's themes, do appear in postmodern discourse, and the fit is intriguing. David Tracy, in his contribution to the volume *God, the Gift, and Postmodernism*, has helped to bridge this gap in the conversation between conservatism and postmodernism. Within what he calls "radical conservatism," Tracy argues that the idea of fragmentation plays an important role.[28] Cultural fragments manifest a lost time and place whose traces remain in our current world. These fragments are approached by conservatives with "regret and nostalgia."[29] The longing of a conservative thinker is typically for a premodern world. As such, the conservative attitude is countermodern in resisting the antitraditional, and in many ways antihuman, attitudes of the totalizing visions of modernity. Fragments recall a place and time when

27. Ibid., 25. Interestingly, a similar note is struck in a caveat by Father Raymond de Souza, the editor of the journal *Religion and Liberty* from the Acton Institute for the Study of Religion and Liberty in Grand Rapids, Michigan. The Acton Institute stands at a confluence of free-market economics and Catholic social teaching and attempts a difficult task as it "promotes a free society characterized by individual liberty and sustained by religious principles." I (Michael) have written for Acton in the past, and when I was asked to write an article a few years back, I suggested something on Berry. After some initial anxiety about Berry's critical posture toward the free market as embodied in the contemporary global economy, *Religion and Liberty* published my brief article on Berry's notion of limit, with this helpful note from Fr. de Souza:

Michael R. Stevens's article on Wendell Berry will strike some readers as a surprising inclusion here. Mr. Berry is no cheerleader for the free market, and his concern for agricultural communities leads him to be suspicious even of technological advances. But Mr. Berry's concern is about the human ecology of the economy: What effect does our economic life have on the life of community and the cultural norms that encourage the discipline of virtue? Those who promote the efficiency and prosperity of economic liberty cannot neglect such questions, even if they come to different conclusions than Mr. Berry. An economic system is not an end in itself—the good of the human person remains always the end of all systems (16, no. 1 [Winter 2006]: 2).

28. "Fragments: The Spiritual Situation of Our Times," in *God, the Gift, and Postmodernism*, ed. John Caputo and Michael Scanlon (Bloomington: Indiana University Press, 1999), 173.

29. Ibid.

the social fabric was more unified and familial connections more vital. Tracy cites T. S. Eliot as one of the most important example of this type of thinker, one who stands amongst the fragments seeking to find other fragments. In his examination of Eliot, Tracy makes an important point about conservatism so conceived. The counter-modern attitude is not a denial of history, a desire to somehow go back in time. Likewise, there is no attempt simply to reestablish an old metaphysic and its concomitant social order. As Tracy points out in his reading of Eliot's *Four Quartets*, this version of conservatism never arrives at a grand synthesis of these fragments.[30] In the end, no final harmony is produced through the reconciliation of tensions. Rather, Tracy contends, Eliot renews for us an awareness of the *saturated nature* of these fragments. The vitality of the fragments contains resistance to reductionism.

Berry's work is very sensitive to the notion of fragmentation, especially in rural agrarian communities. And with conservatives like Kirk, Berry longs for a lost time and place without surrendering to nostalgia. But Berry's countermodern desires don't center on critical recollections of a paradise abandoned. He assumes that damages and wounds will be present and won't be going away. He also looks to the possibilities of healing within a broken present, the struggle underlying the novel *Hannah Coulter*. For Berry, the goodness of creation is never totally obscured, and it keeps recurring, in ways that are surprising, unexpected, but also organic, unforced. So even imperfectly and in the midst of disease one hears the call to health. One can even make judgments of greater or lesser health in the

---

30. It's interesting that Kirk reads Eliot (with whom he was friends and about whom he wrote a whole volume, *Eliot and His Age*) in a similar vein in *The Conservative Mind*, where he notes, "Despite his hesitations and ambiguities, Mr. T. S. Eliot stands in the tradition of Burke and Coleridge; and his books *The Idea of a Christian Society* (1939) and *Notes toward the Definition of Culture* (1948) are among the most significant conservative writings of recent years—the innovator in poetic forms, the weary critic of our wastelands, defending the ideas that nourish civilization" (411). In my own (Michael's) doctoral dissertation work on Eliot's sociopolitical ideas, as revealed through his work as editor of the journal *Criterion* from 1922 to 1939, I found powerful strands of a dynamic, hopeful conservatism: Eliot attended very much to the particulars of time and place in his hopes for a new flourishing of intellectual coherence in the West.

midst of this disease; such judging is in fact always a condition of meaningful human existence. In soil that is damaged and stripped, one can still begin to grow crops that will aid the healing and restoration. Hence, the strange mystery of marriage in the wake of loss, of the sort that brings together Hannah and Nathan Coulter (or my [Matt's] wife Dorothe, a widow when I began dating her, and me). Likewise, our forming of a community-supported agriculture (CSA) farm (in this case Small Wonders Farm—Bonzo and Son, proprietors) doesn't cut our ties to supermarkets, yet the attempt to grow some of our own vegetables has ramifications far beyond the nutritive and economic spheres.

Here Berry seems to have greater similarity with postmodernity than one would expect. Postmodernists too see a kind of countermodernity at work but without a desire for a return or recollection. Responding to Tracy's understanding of Eliot, Jacques Derrida is quick to point out that even the notion of "fragment" implies a totality. Fragments are the remains of a lost unity. Derrida wants to keep all interruptions from being understood as a "broken totality."[31] For the postmodern thinker, there was never a purer time or place. So fragments do not reveal progress or regress. Instead the postmodernists see fragments of a premodern world as a kind of resistance to the totalizing tendencies of modernity; these fragments are extremes that escape capture and containment and represent neither a past nor future synthesis.

Berry's vision, likewise, resists the assumption that big ideas and big movements can somehow capture health. Postmodernity's emphasis on the particular over the universal is mirrored by Berry's privileging of the local over the global. The connections that are the fabric of health and healing can never be virtual for Berry. Both postmodern thinkers and Berry are aware that modernity's totalizing and universalizing systems endanger the local. This can be felt most readily in the damage done to the idea of being "at home." A metaphor for the disease engendered by the "Rational Mind," homelessness—that is, not finding meaning in a particular place—is symptomatic of our age.

31. Caputo and Scanlon, "Derrida's response to Tracy," 181.

Here we can see how Berry's countermodern attitude resonates with a strand of postmodern thought. Berry distrusts big ideas and big movements. His concept of health is not rooted in some totalizing system in which all differences are leveled by "the whole" or "the community." Throughout his writings we are made aware of the tensions and unease generated by human differences. But in his vision even those on the margins of the community are greeted with hospitality. In fact, hospitality is often extended in a more gracious way to the stranger and the unlovely than to members. Through these offers of hospitality, an invitation to join the membership is given, with acknowledgment that the gift need not be accepted. Jayber Crow, appearing in town, is graciously rescued from a flood by Burley Coulter. Later, Mat Feltner's sale of the town barbershop to Jayber is likewise gracious. But Jayber must prove the hospitality is not wasted by entering fully into the life of the community. Such hospitality can be practiced only in a given time and place by a people with a history. And it is through telling stories, which are a kind of fragment of these particular people, that the practice of hospitality continues to be valued. The emphasis postmodernity places on the particular over the universal is again mirrored by Berry's privileging of the local over the remote. The fundamental connections that define health must never be mediated by forces external to the local community.

The unease of negotiating differences within a community is not to be mistaken for the *dis*ease of resolving tensions through dislocation. Countermodern voices are quite attentive to the ways modernity, especially manifest as the global market, endangers the local and erodes a sense of being at home. This erosion is reflected on many levels. The range of analogous uses for *home*, from "being at home in the world" to "being at home in my skin," show that the concern for identity spans from the cosmic to the personal. Modernity's damage to our experiences of being from a particular time and place extends over the entire span of meanings. Whether it is Descartes' call to doubt that the world exists or the global market's demand to be transient for efficiency's sake, we are taught to shun the sort of rootedness that would limit us.

Modernity's warping of boundaries, whether they be physical or spiritual, has led the postmodern self to "find itself ultimately homeless," according to Brian Walsh and Richard Middleton.[32] British sociologist Zygmunt Bauman has noted that in our consumer society, homelessness runs both deep and wide.[33] The analysis offered by these friendly critics of postmodernity is reiterated by Berry. In his essay "The Body and the Earth," he gives an insightful account of the demise of the household as both focus and potential satisfaction move away from the home and toward the marketplace (a critique we'll expand upon in chapter 6). Home is reduced to dwelling, a retreat from "the real world" of the labor market. The house becomes merely a place of convenience and a base for recreational activity. As home becomes house, meaning and identity slip away. Houses and those who dwell in them become interchangeable parts in a bigger system. The ramifications of this movement are vast for Berry. Political and economic life becomes unsustainable without deep roots. Health is, at best, precarious because of the depletion of the ground from which life draws its nutrients.

Obviously, Berry is neither strictly conservative nor strictly postmodern. Our suggestion is bolder in some ways. We think Berry's idea of health and the various themes embedded within it provide a way to address the legitimate concerns of those who hope to counter modernity *either* through a conservative turn to tradition *or* through a postmodern rereading of tradition. That Berry's work can open up such a space for reflection is a powerful validation of his root ideas.

### Berry among the Politicians and Clergy

There is another angle of approach to Berry that we find both surprising and illuminating. Political theorist Jeffrey Stout has argued

32. *Truth Is Stranger Than It Used to Be* (Downers Grove, IL: InterVarsity Press, 1995), 58.

33. Some of Bauman's titles that address this fragmentation include *Alone Again: Ethics after Uncertainty* (London: Demos, 1996) and *Liquid Times: Living in an Age of Uncertainty* (Cambridge: Polity, 2006).

that Berry provides a nexus for strands of sociopolitical thought that might seem utterly divergent. In his 2004 book *Democracy and Tradition*, Stout, an advocate for a secular democratic society, compares Berry favorably with the nineteenth-century British social critic William Cobbett, a farmer and social agitator who wrote under the pen name Peter Porcupine while exiled in America. But then Stout goes further, taking to task Alisdair MacIntyre's "rhetoric of ruin and fragmentation" in the social analysis offered in MacIntyre's volume *After Virtue*.[34] Stout suggests,

> Berry's work, not MacIntyre's, is the closest thing to Cobbett's that we have from a living writer. It is, by my lights, a more honest and rigorously conceived body of work than MacIntyre's. It has three sizeable advantages over MacIntyre's: first, by virtue of expressing in a quite beautiful style a profoundly spiritual sensibility; second, by doing so, for the most part, without resorting to cant or posturing; third, because it includes both *The Unsettling of America* and *The Hidden Wound*, respectively the most important book on environmental ethics ever written and the best book on race that I know of by a white writer. The point to draw attention to here, however, is that Berry's work, with its open embrace of both traditionalist and democratic elements, exists at all, or rather that in exists *in democratic modernity*.[35]

That first advantage, the assertion of Berry's "profoundly spiritual sensibility," reveals another failure of late modern political discourse (though not a failure of Alisdair MacIntyre, we would argue), the demand for a self-policing of one's religious convictions in the political arena. Even Stout, a proponent of the secular sensibilities by which he believes democracy flourishes, recognizes in Berry's account of the essential links of spiritual and social order something that is not only tolerable but necessary for the fully fledged, virtuous *polis*.

34. Jeffrey Stout, *Democracy and Tradition* (Princeton, NJ: Princeton University Press, 2004), 134.
35. Ibid.

Ironically, Stout has recognized a weight and presence to Berry's Christian spirituality that has not been widely noted in the evangelical community. Here he is not without his champions, though much of the impact within evangelicalism has been in pastoral theology and moral discourse. Eugene Peterson has noted his debt to Berry in *Under the Unpredictable Plant*: "Wendell Berry is a writer from whom I have learned much of my pastoral theology. Berry is a farmer in Kentucky. On this farm, besides plowing fields, planting crops, and working horses, he writes novels and poems and essays. The importance of place is a recurrent theme—place embraced and loved, understood and honored. Whenever Berry writes the word *farm*, I substitute *parish*; the sentence works for me every time." Peterson then makes an interesting extension that seems a chastening word to contemporary notions of ministry: "One thing I have learned under Berry's tutelage is that it is absurd to resent your place: your place is that without which you could not do your work. Parish work is every bit as physical as farm work. It is *these* people, at *this* time, under *these* conditions."[36]

Kyle Childress, the pastor of a small church in Nagodoches, Texas, has experienced a similar pastoral vitalization, which he has explored in a 2005 *Christian Century* article: "At denominational meetings and around town I'm asked, 'When are you going to a bigger church? Why do you stay?' Sometimes I give a long, rambling explanation, but often I respond with, 'Because I read too much Wendell Berry.' "[37] Pointing to Berry's patience in trying to restore and heal damaged land, Childress shows the rich metaphorical possibilities for ministry: "We all have church members whose lives are deeply scarred by bitterness, anger, hurt, abuse, disease and death. Add to that the deep scarring caused by war, consumer capitalism, nationalism and racism. In short, scarred by sin. For the gospel of Jesus Christ to grow and heal such worn-out, eroded lives takes patient, long-suffering,

---

36. "Finding the Road to Nineveh," in *Under the Unpredictable Plant: An Exploration in Vocational Holiness* (Grand Rapids: Eerdmans, 1992), 131. Our thanks to Pastor Bob Manuel for pointing out this passage for us.

37. Kyle Childress, "Good Work: Learning about Ministry from Wendell Berry," *Christian Century*, March 8, 2005, 28–33.

detailed work. It takes time to cultivate the habits of peacemaking, forgiveness, reconciliation and love where previously violence, mistrust and fear were the norms. It takes time to grow Christians."[38] This is fresh and refreshing language from a man shaped intimately by Berry's accounts of the human self and human thriving.

Contemporary theologian Marva Dawn has also used Berry's ideas widely in her thinking about countercultural modes of Christian living. She, like Peterson, has found in his vision of community the contours of language that help her articulate what she wants to say about the church in North America.[39]

Such applications of Berry's ethos to pastoral ministry show the strength of his vision of health. The one danger we might see here is the possibility of overspiritualizing his very deliberate social and political aims. His work does speak to the pastoral, as that word's etymological root would suggest. We have several pastor friends who have committed themselves to reading through Berry's fiction, and each has discovered strong resonances with the life of spiritual shepherding. The care for a given community, located and humanized, seems to be a natural extension of Berry's vision.

However, in the evangelical community at large Berry's name remains more or less unknown (or, if known, mistrusted)—he is not on the map with Rick Warren or Chuck Colson as a voice of the social imagination of the church. His contrariness, his rough edges (rife in the essays and present in many ways even in the fiction), may keep him forever on the margins of any audience that too eagerly seeks rational certainty and genial affirmation.

Before we move on, there is one more set of interpreters that we need to preemptively address: the small but persistent company of those who dismiss Berry as an idealist, caught up in a dangerous nostalgia for an agrarian past that never was and can never be. To them we respond: if Berry's vision for life is resonant with creational

38. Childress, 28.

39. See especially her essay "Being Church, Building Community," in *A Royal Waste of Time: The Splendor of Worshipping God and Being Church for the World* (Grand Rapids: Eerdmans, 1999).

themes such as wholeness, community, and love, and if the particularity and humility of his embodied philosophy is magnetic for persons espousing such a wide range of ideologies, then why is he still criticized for representing a deceptive nostalgia? Berry is not calling for everyone to purchase a small farm and a team of mules in order to qualify as a whole human being. But Berry really does believe that the way of life he has chosen is better than the way of life chosen (or accidentally stumbled into) by most other people in America. He really does believe a deliberate, interconnected, and communal (dare we say *democratic*?) local existence is the healthiest mode for human beings. This is because the virtues and habits that he holds up as healthiest and most affirming are most easily seen, most simply practiced, in such a setting. His sharp criticisms of the institutionalized, industrialized, homogenized nature of contemporary American society are meant to offend and perhaps to awaken consciences about the damage done to life by modernity. But there is also sufficient hopefulness, and a sufficient range of ways to undo the damage, at both personal and communal levels.

We will now proceed to trace the shape of Berry's critique in order to show the complex and comprehensive nature of modernity's damage. We do this as insiders, as part of the damage, so that we can hopefully avoid the posture of bringing ready-made solutions. We seek to mimic Berry's own stance, right in the middle of the fray. As we turn to the paradoxes that Berry discerns at various levels of culture, we will begin to see the persistent problems and maybe to glimpse persistent paths of hope.

# 3

............

# The Mad Farmer as Social Critic

## The Painful Path to Healing

If the space between disease and health is the particular territory of Berry's thoughts, what are the implications of his concentration on this "middle ground"? For one thing, he can afford to be patient, frequently hopeful without false exuberance. This patience by which health is fostered requires a turning away from all quick cures or "ready made enlightenment."[1] It's the sort of patience that Berry suggests in his poem "Marriage," as an admission that pain and incompleteness can be present even within a healing love that emerges in the final lines:

> It is to be broken. It is to be
> torn open. It is not to be
> reached and come to rest in
> ever. I turn against you,
> I break from you, I turn to you.
> We hurt, and are hurt,
> and have each other for healing.
> It is healing. It is never whole.[2]

1. Walter Lowe, *Theology and Difference: The Wound of Reason* (Bloomington: Indiana University Press, 1993), 3.
2. "Marriage," in SP, 31.

Likewise, in "The Slip," Berry uses a flood-ravaged riverbank as a metaphor for the wounded soul's recovery:

> There is nothing
> to do but learn and wait, return to work
> on what remains. Seed will sprout in the scar.
> Though death is in the healing, it will heal.[3]

Patience, finitude, hope amidst fragments—these become our watchwords for healing.

For Berry, such openness to pain is the furthest thing from disease. The vulnerable, provisional nature of health in the fallen world is not counter to hope, but it does buttress against an obsession with progress. In "The Agrarian Standard," Berry says, "I have never doubted for a minute the importance of the hope I have tried to serve: the hope that we might become a healthy people in a healthy land."[4] Yet in this provisional world, it is easy to mistake disease for health, at least on the surface of things. This is why Berry often cautions against any suggestion of arrival or completion of healing; for him, language of totality is a sure sign of confusion. For a culture that worships immediacy, Berry's insistence on slowing down, preparing the ground for seeds of hope, is a sharp and persistent counterpoint.

Certainly a measure of caution is needed to judge between health and disease; Berry has often noted how many of the trappings of the culture of death in highly developed nations can appear, at first glance, to be life-giving. Indeed, the commitment to seemingly infinite economic choice has led to a level of consumer frenzy that has captured the imaginations of not only the developed world but the entire global landscape. When promises are disembodied, idealized, dislocated, and generic, they create a deceptive sense of fulfillment. This is the trap into which Jack Beechum falls in *The Memory of Old Jack* when, at his wife's behest, he begins to long for an imaginary

3. "The Slip," in SP, 120.
4. CZP, 143.

landlordship and loses the satisfaction he once felt in his own well-kept little farm.

Berry identifies this misbegotten impulse in "Discipline and Hope" as "heavenly aspiration without earthly reconciliation or stewardship."[5] Implicated here is the tendency of our culture to substitute the therapeutic response, with its temporary solutions, for the hard task of healing. The therapeutic promises an elusive cure instead of the more demanding work of care. A society that is willing to seek only "therapy" is willing to live with disease as normative. In such a world it is more convenient to visit the pharmacy than the farm.

So where does this leave us? In a fallen creation, clearly, and in a time when goodness and evil are painfully intertwined. This is a world of confusion, of unintended consequences, a world beyond easy predictability. There is always a place for repentance, a turn toward health, but never an arrival. Health in a fallen world is not nostalgic return, not ossification, but suggestions toward healing, and it often begins with an exposure of disease that has masked itself as health. This fundamental reorientation or renarration goes a long way toward capturing Berry's understanding of healing. But it has certain conditions inherent in the turn: it cannot be a move of self-empowerment but must be a recognition that healing is *given*, a part of creation's givenness, and can never be taken nor earned. Living by this vulnerable and even fragile hope creates a very real dislocation with its call to turn away from societal expectations. At-home-ness will appear to be alien in a culture alienated from home. But it is the only really life-giving option that lies before us.

The fact that Berry speaks in the language of paradox is helpful as we survey the nature of the diseases of our culture—though he is often pessimistic, he is not a pessimist. The way of healing is always suggested, and hope always rings at last, even if the sorry modern state of human affairs seems to have rung a long time, and loudly.

5. CH, 137.

## Three Orders of Creation Where Health and Disease Are at War

Now we begin to offer an overlay, an interpretive framework, that will hopefully help to explicate Berry's critique. We will seek to show how the fundamental paradox of health and disease works along lines of the *order of knowing*, the *social order*, and the *order of persons*. We are not formally addressing questions of spheres and sphere sovereignty—we've only rather crudely separated these out along Berry's lines of interest, and there are much more subtle, and very important, ways to address this, especially from the perspective of the role of the church and the role of the polis.

But what about these three layers? They are different, but only in degree. The terms and conditions differ, but the imperative toward healing is the same. The movement from the realm of ideas to the social realm to the personal realm arises out of Berry's concern with the particular results of large and abstract notions—particular both in societal changes and in individual lives and places. There is a funneling of sorts here, a raising of the stakes, as we follow his movement from the abstract down to the embodied, since it is the crisis of the particular person in a particular place, right now, that is at the heart of Berry's lament. In chapters 5 and 6, we will reverse the direction, and show the path toward healing communities that Berry offers, from the ground up. For now, it will be enough if we can show both the magnitude and the contours of the crisis. We begin, then, at the abstract level, with more of Berry's critique of the "two minds," the rational and sympathetic. The world constructed by the rational mind is precisely one that claims completion through absolutization and reduction. No human being is outside its purview, nor safe from its peril.

### The Order of Knowing

Thought, creativity, imagination, and even speculation all have appropriate roles in healthy human activity. The problem that can develop, though, is a detachment and uprooting of these ideas from a location within the vital connections of life. Abstract thought becomes dangerous when it fails to recognize its limits, when it fails to recognize itself as human and tries instead to become metaphysical.

If Berry's argument in "The Two Minds" can be taken as a test case for the health of the intellectual order, then the paradigm unfolds like this: The creational order is the only comprehensive order of things. Hence all human attempts at ordering the world are limited in their scope: "The safe competence of human work extends no further, ever, than our ability to think and love at the same time."[6] When we understand ourselves to be atemporal and not particular, we are set up for significant negative surprises when our order fails. Berry includes among these surprises ozone holes, mad cow disease, and the events of 9/11. In a complexly ordered creation, even the best of our abstract insights have unintended consequences. The tremendous efficiency sought through feeding beef products indirectly to our cattle leads to an ugly reality.

The thinking processes involved in attempts to improve our state in the world are not inherently evil, but neither are they inherently good. The question is not *whether* humans order—we order things necessarily as part of our humanness—but really *how* we order things. Do we order with a recognition of a greater order, or do we simply try to impose our order upon the world? How can we give an account for both the healing and the diseased effects of our actions? Since the rise of modern autonomy, since at least Descartes or Francis Bacon, there has been confusion about how we should treat the boundaries of this ordering. The "Rational Mind" tends to hide behind massive, vague concepts such as efficiency and predictability. Such a mind refuses to see, touch, taste, smell, or feel the world in which it acts.

Hyper-efficiency has even reached into such a central and sacred ritual of the church as Communion. Churches can purchase prefilled juice cups, each with a wafer of bread affixed to its top—a prebaked Host reminiscent of nothing so much as a Hostess snack cake. Packaging the Eucharist for ease of delivery seems to countermand

6. CZP, 104.

everything that the Communion table is meant to represent for the believer: reflection, confession, celebration, togetherness.

The dangers of abstracting human things beyond human boundaries are exemplified by Berry in "Sex, Economy, Freedom, Community," where he identifies the contemporary individual as one who "is free to pursue self-realization, self-aggrandizement, self-interest, self-fulfillment, self-enrichment, self-promotion, and so on. The problem is that—unlike a married couple, a household, or a community—one individual represents no fecundity, no continuity, and no harmony. The individual life implies no standard of behavior or responsibility."[7] Thus, attempts to particularize each person's freedoms end in sterile sets of autonomous beings. The masking of disease as health here is particularly deceptive, since few people want to condemn the notion of individual liberty, yet "there is a paradox in all this, and it is as cruel as it is obvious: as the emphasis on individual liberty has increased, the liberty and power of most individuals has declined."[8] As image-bearing has been lost in the definitions of modern autonomy, the built-in limits that afford health have been erased. We end up trying to bear the false god of our own image, our own measure of health and life, which is a way of death. From within a paradigm where there is no standard of behavior or responsibility, it becomes impossible to differentiate between health and disease. Is the quest for economic growth an unproblematic good? Will new school buildings and technologically laden curricula produce better students? Will larger, more "relevant" churches shape more faithful followers? Hidden behind these abstractions is the longing for a self-protective and self-projecting version of success. But when we are solely interested in ordering the world for our benefit, care and connection become obsolete. An abstracted "individual," though prosperous, educated, and thoroughly religious, is likely to be profoundly lonely. Seemingly good ideas thus bear vile fruit, or none at all.

This confusion within the order of knowing is also illuminated by Berry through another contrast, the "cultural landscape" versus the

7. ACP, 162.
8. Ibid., 163.

"actual landscape." With the "cultural landscape" our impression upon creation becomes impositional; we begin to see the "objective, analytical, and empirical"[9] part of us as adequate for comprehending (and thus supplanting) the created order. The "actual landscape," in contrast, is a place "which is always going to be, to some degree, a mystery, from time to time surprising us."[10] In our vulnerability we can discover these pleasant surprises as gifts, given and received as the source of our place in creation. My (Matt) attempts at farming a bit of the actual landscape of Newaygo County, Michigan, have occurred in the midst of a melee in my small community regarding land "development." I now know as much about "site condominiums" as many a suburban planner, though looking at a grid of housing lots is only contemplating an abstraction, a shadow of actually knowing a landscape, a field, and what the soil will grow.

Berry wonders whether the free-standing Rational Mind has any place within it for care or connection, since it is "preoccupied with the search for a sure way to avoid risk, loss, and suffering."[11] On the other hand, the Sympathetic Mind has the long view that "accepts loss and suffering as the price, willingly paid, of its sympathy and affection—its wholeness."[12] In "The Purpose of a Coherent Community" Berry notes that "we seem to have been living for a long time on the assumption that we can safely deal with parts, leaving the whole to take care of itself."[13] A totalizing urge that doesn't really care what is totaled can only end up tearing apart, never really constructing anything.

This pursuit of dismemberment is aimed to arrive at that which is wholly good, though in a context where good is defined as wholly understandable and predictable. In an actual landscape the parts can remain mysterious, with an awareness, though, of the interconnectedness that can make many parts a whole. Here again, the patchwork quilt emerges as an allusive image—mixed patches of

9. CZP, 88.
10. Ibid., 85.
11. Ibid., 92.
12. Ibid.
13. WI, 77.

good and evil, disease and health. A longing for healing can thus arise, as Berry suggests, in a natural, nonmanipulative way, as "affection for its home place, the local topography, the local memories, and the local creatures."[14]

The most significant flaw of the Rational Mind is that it "does not see itself as existing or working in a context. [It] does not think there is a context until it gets there."[15] It mistakes itself, its own presence, as health. Perceiving only its own image in the world, the Rational Mind fails to see that the image imposed by its ordering wreaks damage. The resulting vision of the world is narrow, self-contained, and self-protective. When an inability to grieve and suffer is seen as a strength, the Rational Mind is further cut off from the possibility of healing.[16] In *Life Is a Miracle*, Berry points out that "reductionism has one inherent limitation that is paramount and that is abstraction: its tendency to allow the particular to be absorbed or obscured by the general."[17] What is lost, among other things, is the "human face," the particularity that makes possible individual decisions and actions, the root of which is love. Love that can be abstracted is no longer love. Actual love helps to bring particulars toward wholeness.

In "The Way of Ignorance" Berry laments, "One of the purposes of objectivity in practice is to avoid coming to a moral conclusion."[18] Here again the "rational mind" works at counterpurposes to its stated end, since in its attempt to know through reduction it loses sight of actual human beings. Berry continues with familiar language in arguing for the opposite: "Sympathy gives us an intimate knowledge."[19] The materialist cannot notice the totality of things, because he has broken things into such small parts that they can't be reassembled, let alone cared for. Marketing strategists who reduce people to equations

14. CZP, 89.
15. Ibid., 91.
16. Jim Olthuis, *The Beautiful Risk* (Grand Rapids: Zondervan, 2001). See 39–52 for the "care, not cure" vision of therapy that Olthuis suggests.
17. LM, 39.
18. WI, 55.
19. Ibid., 57.

of consumer predictability are party to such an error, just as those who create master strategies for military campaigns dehumanize by making whole populations pins on a map. Health is pursued in a disembodied way; the small parts aren't actual particulars, so they can never add up to a wholeness. What is constructed is only a veneer of reality. This arrogance of the Rational Mind is akin to the arrogance of Romanticism in its rejection of a world that has never really existed—here Berry, who has been charged with being a romantic and a nostalgist, turns the table by showing the nostalgia at the root of the Enlightenment mind.

So at the level where ideas are given confessional direction, at the level of worldview, Berry recognizes the widespread disembodiment of ideas from the world. When one's understanding of creation is disconnected from the source, then the spirit of one's activity is bound to manifest alienation. Since the "spirit of the age" does not seek to attach just to individuals but also to institutions and organizations, Berry's account of disease extends to social structures, tangible relationships within human society. Insofar as ideas have consequences, they serve to shape the reality in which we navigate social relationships.

As difficult as it is to discern things in the realm of the abstract and ideological, it is nevertheless crucial to keep tracing the strands of these "directional forces" in order to know how and why our culture functions as it does. At the levels of social and personal interaction that we'll now discuss, the difficult work of changing lived habits will depend upon appropriate worldview, not seen merely as individual possession but as culture-directing force.

### The Social Order

What happens when abstract forces begin to take root and bring forth their fruits? What perversions of human society and discourse are thus embodied? Interestingly, in "The Way of Ignorance" Berry uses the term "corporate mind" as an analogue for the Rational Mind, which helps us shift to such embodying at the "social level." When the "Mad Farmer" persona in Berry's poetry declares his independence from just such a mindset in "The Mad Farmer Liberation Front," he is ranting against the embodiment of Rational Mind, which tends to "Love the quick profit, the annual raise / vacation with pay. Want more / of everything ready-made."[20] As a countermeasure, Berry often concentrates his essays on economic and political manifestations in culture—spheres of tangible human interaction. By directing these orders, the ideas of the Rational Mind become embodied and fleshed out in "the corporate mind [which], on the contrary, justifies and encourages the personal mind in its worst faults and weaknesses, such as greed and servility, and frees it of any need to worry about long-term consequences. For these reliefs, nowadays, the corporate mind is apt to express noisily its gratitude to God."[21] The corporate mind of "truth, justice and the American way," that sings the praises of American exceptionalism as divine ordination, thus seeks to create a unified picture, but only by erasing, blurring, and fracturing particular narratives and particular healthy boundaries.

One of Berry's bleak depictions of such a mind comes at the end of the novel *Jayber Crow*, when Troy Keith, the character who seeks progress at any cost, embodied in what he calls the "new farming," lays waste at last to the "Nest Egg," the grove of primeval hardwood trees that has always provided a border to his wife's family's land. This border has been a place of health, a wilderness enclave, and also a place of healing for Mattie, his wife, who must grieve the loss of her children, and for Jayber, who walks with Mattie in these woods from time to time and keeps alive his silent love for her. When Jayber comes upon the scene of destruction, he sees the embodiment, or disembodiment, of the corporate mind:

> I saw us both from a great distance off in time: two small, craving, suffering creatures, soon to be gone. Troy was a beaten man and knew it, and was trying not to know it. You could see it in his eyes. Now at last he was about to inherit a farm that he had worn out, that he had so encumbered with debt that he could not keep it, that I knew

20. SP, 87.
21. WI, 60.

would be dragged into the suck of speculation and development to be sub-divided under some such name as Paradise Estates. This was Troy's last play in what he had sometimes liked to call "the game of farming." What did he have left? Another cutting of timber, maybe, if he could wait another hundred or two hundred years.[22]

Showing the tragedy of such attitudes as Troy's, Berry consistently invites us to look at our social functions through a lens other than utility. Perhaps sustainability (a term of choice across several spheres of culture) offers a fuller, more far-sighted account of human interactions.

Another provocative way to think about the confusion of health and disease within the "social order" comes in the 1983 essay "Two Economies." Berry begins the piece by relating a conversation with Wes Jackson: Berry had lamented the "money economy," suggesting to Jackson that "an economy based on energy would be more benign because it would be more comprehensive." Jackson's playful (but serious) retort was that the only truly comprehensive economy would be "the Kingdom of God."[23] The Kingdom of God is an economy of hope, characterized by an order that is vast and mysterious. This is not merely a theological concept but a reality, present in the world, made of people in places in time! Far from being an abstraction, it is the embodiment of proper relationships:

> The first principle of the Kingdom of God is that it includes everything; in it, the fall of every sparrow is a significant event. We are in it whether we know it or not and whether we wish to be or not. Another principle, both ecological and traditional, is that everything in the Kingdom of God is joined both to it and to everything else that is in it; that is to say, the Kingdom of God is orderly. A third principle is that humans do not and can never know either all the creatures that the Kingdom of God contains or the whole pattern or order by which it contains them.[24]

22. JC, 360.
23. Ibid., 219.
24. Ibid., 220.

The notion of reality bound in mystery becomes a beautiful embodiment, a connection throughout the social order of not only people but also things.

It is within this conversation about the social order, and not the abstract order, that Berry first appeals to the Kingdom of God. For him, clearly, the Kingdom of God is neither purely conceptual nor purely futuristic nor purely otherworldly; rather, the Kingdom points to the actual order of things, which must be reckoned with for anyone to live in reality. Thus, the Kingdom of God seems synonymous with the "culture of health and life" that is at the center of our quest, although the mystery that infuses creation also keeps us from claiming to know the Kingdom's height, breadth, and depth too precisely.

Over against the fabric of this Kingdom of God economy (which Berry calls the "Great Economy,") the absolute economy reveals its disease by constantly reinventing (and dismantling) its basis. Whatever works to undergird constant and unbounded growth is embraced. This protean posture, this intentional flux, is often mistakenly seen as an appropriate stance in a rapidly changing world. There is always the suggestion of a new center, whether it be a "money economy," an "energy economy," or, as Berry suggests here, an "industrial economy."[25] We might go further and include the "global economy," the "information economy," the "consumptive economy," and perhaps even the "leisure economy." The link among all these is their reach toward totalization—though Berry is quick to point out that "the thing that troubles us about the industrial economy is exactly that it is not comprehensive enough, that, moreover, it tends to destroy what it does not comprehend, and that it is *dependent* upon much that it does not comprehend."[26]

The disease of the absolute economy is its belief that it is in control. So wisdom is reduced to technique: pulling the right levers to create control. This is exemplified in the aforementioned crisis in *The Memory of Old Jack*, when Jack Beechum is seduced away

25. Ibid., 219.
26. Ibid.

from his better judgment by the possibility of expanding his holdings and "conquering" the adjoining farm. The fuel for his mania is in part his wife's desire to find conventional prosperity in land ownership, but Jack finds that the price, both monetary and psychological, is destructive. We see Jack embodying the ironic enslavement that comes from seeking a freedom beyond boundaries. The pain is extended when Jack's daughter Clara ends up marrying a man, the Louisville banker Glad Pettit, who utterly devalues the land by seeing it simply in monetary value. This commodification is a diseased outworking of control, though here, as elsewhere, control serves as the mask of health: the abstract ordering leads to disordering at the concrete level, so that Jack is forced to live sternly on the outside, always harboring within himself his bitterness.

In "The Two Economies" Berry points explicitly to the destructive nature of this strategy by calling it the "explosive economy,"[27] one that sets in motion processes that are destructive if not limited, and that are controlled yet that can't *be* controlled. What starts off as an attempt to control Nature ends up as a turn against Nature, a destructiveness no less insidious for being myopic and accidental.

In contrast, the "Great Economy" manifests itself in humility and littleness, in a particularity of scope. Health is measured here not in terms of bounty and productiveness but in terms of good work and good habits: "When the virtues are rightly practiced within the Great Economy, we do not call them virtues; we call them good farming, good forestry, good carpentry, good husbandry, good weaving and sewing, good homemaking, good parenthood, good neighborhood, and so on."[28] The way toward this healing, then, is again the local, the finite, the particular. Berry suggests, "For a human, the good choice in the Great Economy is to see its membership as a neighborhood and oneself as a neighbor within it."[29] Further, he asserts, "Competitiveness cannot be the ruling principle, for the Great Economy is

27. Ibid., 231.
28. ACP, 234. Also, in the volume *The Gift of the Good Land*, Berry includes a few essays that narrate the work of farmers doing restorative work on depleted land ("Seven Amish Farms") and on formerly strip-mined land ("A Rescued Farm").
29. ACP, 234.

not a 'side' that we can join nor are there such 'sides' within it. Thus, it is not a 'sum of its parts' but a *membership* of parts inextricably joined to each other, indebted to each other, receiving significance and worth from each other and from the whole. One is obliged to 'consider the lilies of the field,' not because they are lilies or because they are exemplary, but because they are fellow members and because, as fellow members, we and the lilies are in certain critical ways alike."[30] Berry shows that the Kingdom of God is not an oppositional stance to the world or a linear, conquering force in the world, but rather an understanding of the fundamental kinships by which we can foster life in the world. The self always has a bigger circle, a bigger context in which to dwell. Whereas disembodied abstractions lead us nowhere, embodied relationships lead toward true human flourishing. As we recognize and respect these kinships and live joyfully within their limits, healing can occur.

What does this look like when it comes to cases in the social order? The contrast of industrialism to agrarianism is, for Berry, far more than just a play between differing views on agriculture versus manufacturing. The integrity of the Kingdom of God is at stake here, because the choice is not economic so much as directional, a choice between particularizing to individual human selves or totalizing toward control of whole systems, toward institutionalization of power. "If we do not serve what coheres and endures, then we serve what disintegrates and destroys."[31] The disease of industrialism is an attempt by humans at ordering things by their own power. But this ordering has no antecedent, no creational limits, and so it is imaginary, often virtual, with no actual human relationships at the bottom of the cycle. Instead, the end is always cast in terms of efficiency, which can be temporarily productive but not life-sustaining.

In his essay "A Nation Rich in Natural Resources," Berry argues, "The industrial economy, on the other hand, reduces the value of a thing to its market price. . . . But when nothing is valued for what it is,

30. Ibid., 233.
31. Ibid., 235.

everything is destined to be wasted."[32] The result of such reduction and waste is not only pollution but placelessness.[33] Berry vividly describes such a decline at the end of the essay: "Once the values of things refer only to their future usefulness, then an infinite withdrawal of value from the living present has begun. Nothing (and nobody) can then exist that is not theoretically replaceable by something (or somebody) more valuable. The country that we had thought to make our home becomes instead 'a nation rich in natural resources'; the good bounty of the land begins its mechanical metamorphosis into junk, garbage, silt, poison, and other forms of 'waste.'"[34] This placelessness leads not only to counterproductive and wasteful habits, like long commutes that drain energy and generation of industrial waste that can never be reused or returned to the earth, but also to the deepest problem, which is a spiritual rootlessness, a homelessness of people's hearts.

The agrarian life is characterized not by efficiency but by belonging, by care-fulness. In "The Agrarian Standard," Berry notes: "If we believe the world is rooted in mystery and in sanctity, then we would have a different economy."[35] Again, the way to healing seems to be through humility, since "our life of need . . . calls for prudence, humility . . . complex responsibilities of caretaking and giving back that we mean by stewardship."[36] To know our place is a humbling embrace of our finitude, but it is also relational. If the chief wound that industrialism leaves is dislocation, then the possibility of healing can come only through the hard work, perhaps even the inefficient work, of homemaking.

### The Order of Persons

Homes can be made, and dwelt in, and shared, only by persons. Here we reach our third level of paradox, as we see Berry wrestling with the question he has so aptly phrased in the title of his

32. HE, 135.
33. See especially the essay "Some Thoughts on Citizenship and Conscience," LLH, 85–86.
34. HE, 136.
35. CZP, 146.
36. Ibid., 147.

1989 volume: *What Are People For?* A primary way of entering this contrast is to look at the difference between the machine and the human. Berry traces a scary reductionism, as outlined in "Health Is Membership": "The 'progress' here is the reduction of mind to brain and then of brain to computer."[37]

Berry's touchstone here, as for all other articulations, is the land. By "land" Berry means foremost the actual soil, the ground under our feet and the ground of which we are made. Early in his writings, in the essay "The Loss of the Future," he already shows this concern: "For man is not merely 'in' the world. He is, he must realize and learn to say or to be doomed, part of it. The earth he is made of bears in trust."[38] We can never remove ourselves and cease to be organic parts of the whole, and so the more that places become interchangeable (or even irrelevant) to the floating individual, the more imperiled personhood becomes.

The connection of people to earth is germane, since Berry finds many of his fundamental contrasts in the organic parlance of farming. In his essay "Conserving Communities," he offers a most basic contrast between machines and people: "If you have eyes to see, you can see that there is a limit beyond which machines and chemicals cannot replace people; there is a limit beyond which mechanical and economic efficiency cannot replace care."[39] He is clear that "the way of industrialism is the way of the machine."[40] This is the way for such antiheroes of Berry's fiction as Glad Pettit and Troy Chatham, and it invites the lingering (and haunting) questions raised by the novel *Hannah Coulter*: Does anything survive after mechanization? Why do we seem to end up as dismembered individuals, disconnected from the community by means of the very technology that was supposed to give us more time with each other? And what do we learn from Berry's positing of "the Membership of Port William" over against the dismemberment?

37. ACP, 149.
38. LLH, 63.
39. ATC, 111.
40. CZP, 144.

One kind of dismemberment arises from the idealization of competition, and Berry takes this version of disease to task in his essay "Economy and Pleasure." At the personal level, the mask of pleasure and comfort hides a destructive exploitation. Here the problem is defined as different understandings of pleasure. The pseudo-pleasure invoked by the competitive spirit in the form of titillation always comes at the expense of community and is the fruit of a culture of narcissism. The pleasure arising from competition can easily end up dividing and excluding, because it is always at the expense of another, always a breach of kinship.

To be at home in creation is to forgo competition as the modus operandus for living: "It is equally obvious that no individual can lead a good or satisfying life under the rule of competition, and that no community can succeed except by limiting somehow the competitiveness of its members."[41] The pleasure arising in the proper context of community is oriented outside of self and toward others, and ultimately toward God. We orient ourselves the context of God's pleasure, and thus our pleasure is never an end in itself, never narcissistic, but always interpersonal. Sharing our resources and ourselves, we give and receive communal pleasure as gift, and there we come to an appropriate sort of individual pleasure. This is a healing pleasure.

The healing path is thus to see things in their particularity and limitedness, while always recognizing that God's creation is mysterious and irreducible, more than we can see or know. Frugality, thrift, and economy are virtues that find their proper exercise in a recognition of needs expressed and met within the creation order. Within a membership, frugality does not become miserliness and thrift doesn't lapse into greed; instead of turning inward, these virtues reach outward, seeking the well-being of the membership. Only in that communal well-being does each person find his or her pleasure. Pleasure can never be a dis-located experience.

In the poem "The Satisfactions of the Mad Farmer," Berry addresses the creational pleasures appropriate to the human being, and

41. ACP, 211.

they are unfailingly communal: "the work of feeding and clothing and housing, / done with more than enough knowledge / and with more than enough love, / by men who do not have to be told."[42] This literal husbandry is a beginning of coherent order, and husbandry well exercised is a frugality that fosters rather than hoards life. In his essay "Renewing Husbandry" Berry parses out the verb form this way: "to husband is to use with care, to keep, to save, to make last, to conserve."[43] It requires a delicate balance: the community's membership is protected by a frugality that is directed toward the common good—and hence back toward each person. Berry continues in "The Purpose of a Coherent Community": "The members of community cohere on the basis of their recognized need for one another, a need that is in many ways practical but never utilitarian."[44] In this communal context of personhood, even traits we might associate with an independent, detached individual can serve the greater good. The long poem "Some Further Words," for example, shows that frugality, far from being miserly, can be a spiritual discipline that fosters community: "I think / an economy should be based on thrift, / on taking care of things, not on theft, / usury, seduction, waste, and ruin."[45]

In Berry's fiction, the "qualifications" for membership in the community seem to have much to do with taking care of one's own place and caring about the well-being of other people's places. This charitable thrift is revealed in the reception of Jayber Crow in the community, when he pulls out $200, carefully saved in his shoe, and thus shows Mat Feltner and Burley Coulter that he values the barbershop as more than a speculation. Conversely, characters who are careless with their belongings and relationships are shown to be unworthy of membership because of selfishness. The McGrother family, the evil neighbors of Jack Beechum in *The Memory of Old Jack*, use and abuse the land, animals, and each other—to the disgust of Jack, a conscientious farmer.

42. CP, 132.
43. WI, 96–97.
44. Ibid., 79.
45. GP, 30.

To say that the basic problem for the person in our world is a spiritual one is not to say that it is otherworldly or disconnected from the earth; it is not to abstract it at all. Ideas are important: they undergird the social systems and structures in which individuals live and work and find meaning. Breakage and confusion in our ideas and our spiritual practice lead to human hurt. Berry reveals the failure of abstraction, the failure of social systems predicated upon abstraction, and the failure of abstracting human beings. But he also points us to hope.

# Human Responsibility and the Enduring Goodness of Creation

Much of the charm and persuasion of Berry's work lies in the simplicity with which he reads the world. Yet if we are going to read him through the lens of Christian confession, at times we need to make use of somewhat technical language and concepts to clarify the tensions present not just in his work, but in any earnest struggle with the narrative of creation, fall, and redemption. The "given creation" is good and worthy of our care, Berry argues, yet it is also fallen, diseased, unhealthy, and thus longing for redemption. Berry shows that we need not sit by passively, waiting for redemption to happen. To probe his thinking further, here we will introduce the language of *structure* and *direction*.

Having considered the power of Berry's vision, its attractiveness to a wide-range of thinkers, its countercultural weight and current, its thoroughgoing critique of disease at various levels of human existence, we need to ask whether the vision is cohesive, rooted in a story that holds the various pieces together. We suggest that Wendell Berry offers an account of the world that resonates deeply with the biblical narrative.

Berry's vision is at its heart confessional; this seems clear from any angle. Would it do to call it a worldview? Philosopher Calvin Seerveld distinguishes between "worldview," which he sees as "pre-theoretical," and the "world and life vision": a "vision of everything all together, which is imaginative and literarily suggestive in quality rather than theoretically precise, which structures and can guide one's concrete experience in God's ordered cosmos."[1] Seerveld's definition avoids the totalizing, overly intellectual understanding that is in many quarters a synonym for apologetics. His definition is congruent with Berry's patchwork vision, which is best construed as lived existence, with a nearly infinite range of shapes provided by imagination but decidedly finite with reference to creational givens. For farmers, for example, there are myriad combinations of crops and livestock that can constitute a livelihood, but soil and weather will always limit what the land can offer.

Berry's triad of health-disease-healing resonates strongly with the Reformed worldview motif of creation-fall-redemption. "Health" is Berry's aspiration for the world "as it should be," the wholeness and abiding goodness that is the object of all true longing. With "disease" Berry points to the displacement, disconnection, and dis-orientation that we must struggle against at every juncture, lest we be moved away from God, the earth, and ourselves. "Healing" involves recounting what has been lost and reconciling our fragmented selves to both Creator and creation. Healing is a progression toward an end: wholeness. This is an eschatological vision, though not a millenarian one; the concern is not with the nature of the "last days" but with the fulfillment of creation. In applying the term *eschatology* to Berry's vision, we are concerned not so much with the present giving way to the future as with the way the future is made known in the present.

Berry himself has shown little interest in conceptualizing and working out the theoretical implications of his vision. The work of the Reformed scholar Al Wolters, however, can help with such a systematic

1. Calvin Seerveld, "The Damages of a Christian Worldview," paper presented at After Worldview Conference, Cornerstone University, Grand Rapids, MI, September 2004, 2.

examination. Wolters's insight into the creation-fall-redemption motif is laid out in his book *Creation Regained*. He draws a crucial distinction regarding the order of creation, which he casts in terms of "structure" and "direction." "Structure refers to the order of creation, to the constant creational constitution of anything, what makes it the thing or entity that it is."[2] This notion of *structure* provides a double boundary: the norms of creation and, because of the fall, the extent of corruption. Structure "calls" the actual into existence by establishing the conditions for that existence. The soil's ability to produce vegetative life, for example, is part of its creational call, its structure, but this structure can be violated, such as by heavy application of herbicide. Such violation, often done in the name of efficiency, brings dire consequences both to the soil and to the web of life that depends on it. Similarly, for human beings the structure of family provides normative nurturing, and the disintegration of family brings tragic consequences. With both of these examples, structure never disappears; even where it has been violated, the calls for the soil to bring forth life and for the family to nurture remain present.

Enduring goodness cannot be eradicated by sin. This notion of structure is echoed in Berry's idea of creation as "the given," which burgeons with goodness. The suggestion of right and proper boundaries as life-giving also coheres with this sense of structural shape. But structure is not an idealized blueprint that is simply duplicated throughout creation. It is more like a call and response. Berry's notion of the local and the particular resonates with the idea of "call": the structure is not an otherworldly reality, static and abstract, but dynamic, a lived experience. Farming in Kentucky is different from farming in Peru—the topography, the soil, the customs, weather, history, stories are all quite different—but if the farmer in each place desires to cultivate living things, there are ways to act in accord with the structure of that place.[3]

*Direction*, then, denotes whether the embodied response to the "call" of the structure is obedient or disobedient to God's

2. Albert Wolters, *Creation Regained* (Grand Rapids: Eerdmans, 1985), 49.
3. See especially Berry's essay "An Agricultural Journey in Peru" in GGL.

intent, whether it brings life or death. Wolters says, "Anything in creation can be directed either toward or away from God, that is, directed either in obedience or disobedience to his law. To the degree that these realities fail to live up to God's creational design for them, they are misdirected, abnormal, distorted."[4] Berry's term for such failure is generally "diseased," pointing to a human role, a place for choice between acceptance and rejection of given boundaries.

## Linear and Cyclical Visions of Life

Berry's vision is often expressed in the language of *gift* and *givenness*. Structure is the boundedness that is built into creation, boundaries that call not for lament but humility and proportionality. But structure is also God's gift to us, his love embodied, and calls for our gratitude. Controlling, overcoming, superseding—all these are destructive impulses toward violating structural limits. Structure is the fundamental "given thing," given not as a blueprint but as a call and response. It requires human negotiation for its fulfillment, for fruitfulness and health—Genesis 2:15 can, in fact, be read as a trope for "farming." It is always necessary for human beings to work at the creational structure's unfolding; humans can't avoid guiding creation, because all of our actions are directional. We either foster life or foment disease, or most likely do some measure of both, whenever we act in this fallen world. Human actions always take place within the context of a creation that is open; creation may be thought of as fully healthy not when empty from humans but when appropriately stewarded and nurtured by people. Berry's work consistently points out that we always have an effect upon the rest of creation, often at multiple levels, just by virtue of being humans. His concern is primarily the danger of denying that we have an impact, but he also warns against the claim that we need not recognize natural limits just because we have the apparent power to supersede them.

4. Wolters, *Creation Regained*, 49.

Berry recognizes a responsibility that does not end, a faithful stewarding that is ongoing between the given and the gifted. This negotiation with limits is at the heart of his understanding of farming, of household, of community, and of patriotism. Direction has to do with faithfully directing creation in light of the conditions and choices that come out of Genesis 3—the fall is always present, alongside creation's goodness. Before the fall, there was only one direction chosen—faithfulness. But the fall has damaged our ability to respond to the structures of creation. Our vision is clouded, and hence the attraction of the "quick fix" that would seem to solve our dilemmas immediately. The curse of disobedience is manifested in the struggle associated with our work to bring forth life. This situation does not call for despair or nostalgia, whether for "idyllic childhood" or for Eden, nor for escape into a world of fantasy. Instead, the faithful path is one of oft-frustrated hopefulness, a sensibility that can wed grief with joy. This long journey, this life's work, is what Berry seeks to embody in his own and his characters' commitment to place and people.

Berry is rightfully hesitant to overemphasize ungrounded speculation; conversation about the land or the community that is abstract is likely going to do more harm than good. This is why Berry is cautious to expand upon the eschatological nature of creation, since cosmic fulfillment, the "Kingdom come," is an end that can be gotten at only through faithful living in the here and now. Eschatology for him is not useful for jumping ahead to the end of the story but rather for acting with a purpose within the story. In my (Matt's) experience as a fowler—that is, raising a bunch of unruly chickens—I've learned the truth of "not counting your chickens before they hatch," since not only do we eat most of the eggs, but chickens lead perilous lives, both in and out of the shell. The work of chicken raising can never be purely oriented toward the future but must be enacted each day in the stewarding of the flock.

The fine line here seems to be how we might live within limits without surrendering our initiative to creatively follow our calling. If structure offers us the limits that can yield health, we must still pursue directional flourishing—there is no life in a static creation. The recognition that we live within limits is what we call *finitude*; creational boundaries help shape the outline of who we are and who we're supposed to be. The call is always to be fully human by recognizing, respecting and responding from within these limits. However, *fallenness* is distinct from finitude; it involves transgression of limits through misdirection, through disobedience to the call. Though not using these terms, Berry emphasizes this distinction whenever he laments the pride by which the creature, wishing to undo the conditions of both fallenness and creaturehood, aspires to be Creator and thus brings disease and ruin. Berry notes in "The Way of Ignorance" that "we are more destructive now than we've ever been, because of our ignorant and arrogant use of knowledge."[5]

Another way to get at this distinction is to identify the limits imposed by the fall as *self-enclosure*: sin brings the misplacing of the self in creation. This enclosure, which seems to offer self-assurance, proves lethal because it cuts off the possibility of receiving gifts and prevents hospitality and healing. The limits of our creatureliness, on the other hand, constitute appropriate boundaries, built into the structure of creation, and recognizing them is necessary for healthy self-understanding and connection with both God and others. Within the fallen creation, we find ourselves caught in a tension. We confront, on the one hand, healthy boundaries that can be recognized only in obedience—for instance, a desire to create sustainable food systems requires a recognition of boundaries of place and people. Growing the kinds of food that a given soil can sustain long term must dictate culinary choices—beans are easier on the earth than corn (though not as tasty, some might say!). As Berry himself points out, certain breeds of sheep tend to thrive on the Kentucky hillsides—specifically those not given to arthritic knees. On the other hand, we encounter boundaries created by the fall: these can be imagined as blank walls or electric fences, intended to trap us within certain habits, having a deceitful momentum of their own, and offering only the promise of circumventing obedience.

5. WI, 59.

In our obedient response to structure, we create healthy boundaries. In our arrogance, we create chaos under the guise of boundaries, raised precisely to transcend the structure of creation. The crucial act of discerning which boundaries to respect and which to free ourselves from is made exceedingly difficult by the fact that they are often intertwined. Further, it is easy for our responses to become skewed because neither sort of boundary is fully visible; each represents transcendent powers, spiritual forces at work in the world. God's call to obedience is mysterious, not always answerable to logic but always answerable to life. The diabolical call of the "spirits of the age" often seems to point in a rational or intelligible direction, concealing the chaos that can only destroy. The possible erroneous responses thus always have some partial vision of life at the root: a proclivity for instant gratification is rooted in our longing for pleasure; grim fatalism can mask itself as resignation and acceptance; a nostalgic rendering of the past offers the twin bill of idealism and tradition; an ungrounded wish for infinite human progress can run for a long time on the fumes of aspiration; and a focus on purely heavenly bliss has the backing of piety.

A hope rooted in the goodness of creation, which is open to both the past and the future, is a hope made present. The proper response to the limits imposed by the fall is thus to live here and now with an eschatological vision of the Kingdom. Far from nostalgia or wish fulfillment, this means living in a fuller, healthier *reality* than what we can see now. Such a life will be guided by a remembering of creation's goodness and the anticipation of creation's fulfillment. But appropriation of the past and the future in the present can be done only by finite creatures. Our creaturely limits, as Berry doggedly points out, call for us to recognize and submit so as to live within the boundaries, the finitude, the humility that makes healing possible.

So Berry's eschatological vision is born out of a structure that is teleological, a linear progression toward the Kingdom. But he shies away from typical understandings of the linear "myth of progress," and often emphasizes a different shape to his vision, a different concept of time, when he speaks of the fruitfulness of living cycles. His tendency toward cyclical terminology shows his deep attention to our present embodiment within creation. The cyclical image has a natural orientation: things come and go, live and die. There is no sense of an ethereal Neoplatonic cycle of emanation and return. Berry's cycles are seasonal, meteorological, because they are ultimately creational.

In his "Discipline and Hope," Berry suggests that simply following the materialist-linear approach of modernity will mean a trespassing of legitimate structural boundaries, whereas "the cyclic vision, at once more realistic and more generous, recognizes in the creation the essential principle of return: What is here will leave to come again; if there is to be having there must also be giving up. And it sees death as an integral and indispensable part of life."[6] When Berry contrasts the linear and cyclic modes explicitly, he reveals the false transcendence of the linear in its "Heavenly aspiration without earthly reconciliation or stewardship. The creation as commodity." His cyclic perspective doesn't solve the tension between spiritual and material by pulling the heavenly into the earthly in a sort of pantheism. Rather, Berry offers a notion of difference and yet connection, with the eschatological vision offering clarity for the here and now: "Reconciliation of heaven and earth in aspiration toward responsible life. The creation as source *and end*."[7] Here, the creation is the place where life and death are embodied, and the provocative notion of "creation as end" seems to be of creation not as an end unto itself but as the place where the Kingdom will come.

An idealized "linear" projection of the future brings disease, characterized by "Progress. The conquest of nature." Berry's list of contrasts grows pithy, as we find the "linear" characterized by "Training. Programming. / Possession. / Quantity," whereas the "cyclic" is rooted in "Education. Cultural process. / Usufruct, relinquishment. / Quality."[8] The future is either based upon human determination and control or comes to us as gift. The terminology of the latter list is significant: *usufruct* is by definition the use of land not one's own, and hence the notion of *relinquishment* points to givenness, the gift of the land for a time, the relational dynamic that is lost in a focus

6. GGL, 136.
7. Ibid.
8. Ibid.

on "possession" (cf. Lev. 25:23). Inherent in Berry's notion of gift is the notion of limit or call. Hence his emphasis throughout the essay on the centrality of discipline and restraint, both of which follow from a sense of stewardship rather than reckless ownership.

Some might protest that the "cyclic" suggests too confined a vision. Nature's cycles move in an active process, but Berry is wary of the idea of progress toward a finite end. As we've noted, his writing is open to a broader eschatological reading, an openness to receiving God's gift of the future. The future can inform both past and present as an important source of hope. Furthermore, the past finds its proper role as we reject nostalgic visions for the present that are informed only by an idealized past.

## Shrouded Hope

To fully recognize Berry's hope we must first realize that for him, surrender is not despairing. There is a basis for hope in the midst of a fallen creation, because there is a goodness that undergirds and sustains human endeavors. It's just difficult to feel this hope when reality is so misdirected.

Interestingly, Berry's insights into this dynamic have come outside the walls of the church, both literally and metaphorically. The fields have spoken to him much more than has any pastor. The best of Berry's sabbath poems over the years (collected in *A Timbered Choir* and elsewhere) picture the poet walking his land every Sunday morning to glimpse bits of God in the woods and fields—with a tacit alienation from the church as the subtext. In *Jayber Crow*, the title character and narrator, erstwhile seminarian and now town barber, reflects on the many young, transient ministers to serve in Port William, and the failure common to them all: "What they didn't see was that [the world] is beautiful, and that some of the greatest beauties are the briefest. They had imagined the church, which is an organization, but not the world, which is an order and a mystery."[9] This

9. JC, 160.

81

is the lament at the root of the sabbath poems, but it also provides the surprise of seeing God at work in the mystery of creation.

In *Given* selections from the sabbath poems of 1998–2004 show the weariness of efforts to find hope, in tones that are by turns reconciled and angry:

> Nothing
> Is given that is not
> Taken, and nothing taken
> That was not first a gift.
>
> The gift is balanced by
> Its total loss, and yet,
> And yet the light breaks in,
> Heaven seizing its moments
> That are at once its own
> and yours. (Poem VI, 1998)

There is a sustenance in loss, an edification:

> In Heaven the starry saints will wipe away
> The tears forever from our eyes, but they
> Must not erase the memory of our grief. (Poem V, 1999)

So also, in Poem III from 2000, we can find joy in our finitude, as "Longing and dark, / We are completely filled / With breath of love, in us / Forever incomplete." In Poem IX from 2000, love is seen to burgeon in death's shadow:

> I've gone too far toward time,
> And now have come back home.
> I stand and wait for light,
> Flight-weary, growing old,
> And grieved for loss of time,
> For loss of time's gifts gone
> With time forever, taught
> By time a timeless love.

82

The events of September 11, 2001, and the subsequent (ongoing) warfare, touched the sabbath poems with a darker weariness. Poem I of 2002 exemplifies this tone: "Weary, / an old man feeds hay / to the stock at the end / of a winter's day / in a time reduced / to work, hunger, worry, / grief, and as always / war, the killed peace / of the original world." The sabbathscapes are altered, overshadowed, for Berry now, as in Poem III of 2003: "The Lords of War sell the earth to buy fire, / . . . Their intention to destroy any place is solidly founded / upon their willingness to destroy every place." Poem VII from the same year takes the lament even further, into a silence just shy of resignation: "When they cannot speak freely in defiance / of wealth self-elected to righteousness, / let the arts of pleasure and beauty cease." So the loop of eschatological hope sometimes stops short, grinds to a halt in the no-man's-land of this broken world, with no place to turn.

Even in times when hope is most obscured, Berry consistently warns against the temptation to ignore or circumvent or supersede the problem through unbridled power. Equally dangerous would be the tendency to long for the purely good, untouched and unsullied by human desire, an innocent nature that is merely a nostalgic invention. Berry resists all these inadequate responses by the hard labor of wrestling with human responsibility within the tension of goodness and fallenness, health and disease, life and death. If his vision of life is bounded by the reality of death all around, he understands that the sting of death has been ultimately defeated by the hope of redemption and resurrection, the hope of the new creation that cannot be invented or earned but can only be received as the gift of the good Creator.

## Mysterious Hope

Although we will treat Berry's analysis (and our prognosis) for the church in chapter 9, it seems helpful to make a few comments on Berry's structural critique of otherworldly faith. In "Christianity and the Survival of Creation," Berry's reflections on the anticreational orientation of much institutionalized Christianity are rooted in a critique of dualism, of the human as a merely biological entity or as merely a soul sojourning in a body. This is perhaps where the evangelical community should attend most closely to Berry, since the tendency to reject creation as our home leads to dangerous dislocations.

The scriptural notion of "resident alien" is best articulated as a directional homelessness and uneasiness, not a structural alienation. We feel uneasy because creation is misdirected and goodness is hidden. Berry's call to see our human selves as a mystery is thus a call to see ourselves as linked to, limited appropriately by, and fully residing within the creation order. We participate in what is good, and we help enact the healing of what is corrupted in the creation with our hopeful kingdom work. This notion of active resident-alienhood is backed up in "The Burden of the Gospels," where Berry again urges us, via the Gospels, to "the opening of a mystery in which our lives are deeply, dangerously, and inescapably involved."[10]

In "The Gift of the Good Land" Berry is concerned that believers in a creating and gifting God recognize that "the wild ass and the wild lilies are loved by God for their own sake and yet they are part of a pattern that we must love because it includes us. This is a pattern that humans can understand well enough to respect and preserve, though they cannot 'control' it or hope to understand it completely. The mysterious and the practical, the Heavenly and the earthly, are thus joined."[11] If we move away from control, we can't rest at a point of merely taking for granted the creation, since that leads too easily toward subtler forms of use and abuse. How often does our talk of an "appreciation of the earth" become euphemistic for cordoning it off, isolating part of it for our own entertainment and recreation? Is a constructive recreation possible without a prior understanding of creation itself? Is the preservation of a pristine creation, via nature preserves and national parks, the fullest way to reckon with mystery, or does this impulse tend to mask the more

10. WI, 132.
11. ACP, 298.

difficult but far more crucial task of interacting appropriately and healthily with the creation in which we reside?

Berry's critique is a critique of "creation lost" for all of us. We must all deal with the directional confusion both in our tendencies to demystify that which we want to exploit and in the reverse impulse to hyper-mystify so that we as humans are vilified and excluded from nature. Neither the industrial park nor the state park helps us to think fully about healthy connections (although it's certainly easier to contemplate the mystery in a state park than in a factory parking lot). Our place is within the mystery, limited by it but still participating in it. Berry has sought to lay bare the structures that have been given us, that we are called to steward, and that we are to love though we'll never fully understand. He is calling us to live fully and deliberately with mystery, to be shaped by the mystery rather than to solve and shape it. So also the ancient story of scripture shapes us.[12]

But how can the church do its healing, hopeful work when its members continue to see creation as something to master, rather than to nurture? Berry shows in "The Body and the Earth" that we expand our autonomy as we attempt to usurp the role of Creator. The sense of being a creator, of transcending creation, is all-consuming, and so the diminishment of the self toward enslavement is radical and severe: "We became less and less capable of sensing ourselves as small within Creation, partly because we thought we could comprehend it statistically, but also because we were becoming creators, ourselves, of a mechanical creation by which we felt ourselves magnified. . . . And yet these works that so magnify us also dwarf us, reduce to insignificance."[13] Disease comes again in our lack of recognition of limits, of space and time and even mortality. Regarding the last of these, defenders of the Enlightenment project often cite their ultimate goal as the extension of lifespan, the great quantitative leap.

---

12. Rich Mullins's song "The Creed" captures this notion well in the chorus, where he augments his singing of the Apostles' Creed by affirming, "I did not make it, but it is making me."

13. ACP, 96.

Berry addresses this in "Quantity vs. Form": "A good life consists, in part at least, of doing well; and . . . this possibility is an ancient one, having apparently little to do with the progress of science or how much a person knows. And so we must ask how it is that one does not have to know everything in order to do well."[14] "The Body and the Earth" might at first be taken as a harsh critique, but it does help us move forward, to reorient ourselves toward healing, by asking difficult questions: Can an exposure of the dismemberment be the first step toward healing? Can a recognition that the body has no limbs ever lead to wholeness? The vulnerable but necessary answer is "yes." It is a recognition that we have been traveling the way of death; it is repentance. It is this miraculous return toward health, a gift that lies outside the bounds of reductionistic explanation.

If you begin with the idea of creation as gift, as "given," it's purely within Berry's logic of giving to see restoration and healing as possible only within an eschatological hope. Practicing resurrection thus becomes the link of past, present, and future, in a lived and embodied hopefulness, anchored in narratives of the past, partaking of future hope, and living in the goodness of an ordered, "here-and-now" present.

14. WI, 83.

# 5

..............

# The Cultivation of Community
## from the Ground Up

If Wendell Berry has gained a reputation as a contrarian voice (one he might well savor, by the way), that tells only part of the story. His critique of our diseased culture is resounding and blunt, but his thoughts never leave off before pointing to hope, though always bounded hope, with an acute awareness that grief is never distant. His critique, as we've argued, always suggests the sort of action necessary for healing: a reorientation toward health that involves a submission not only to creation order (structure) but also to the narrative of human relationships in which we dwell. And if his essayist voice suggests this, his novelist voice downright declares it, as the characters in the "membership of Port William" make sense, or find sense, only within the broader story of their people and their place.

Stories are foundational to human experience. Before any worldview construction can take place, there must be a story, a narrative that invites human beings into interaction with their world. The scriptures provide for Christianity a root narrative about God's interaction with humankind and all of creation, a narrative that compels its enstoried listeners in certain normative directions.

Berry reminds us that creation itself tells its story through its rhythms and cycles. He is adamant that any discussion of human story that ignores this creational story is destined to be diseased, just as any rejection of God's story is destructive. It's foolhardy to speak of creation without God, and likewise to speak of God apart from creation is dangerously speculative. If we're to begin talking of healing, we must do so within the boundaries of healing narratives in specific times, places, communities, people. In placing his stories so deliberately, Berry reveals the crucial nature of living with a coherent story, where trust, humility, and gratitude link each person to creation, to other people and to God. Even Berry's poems and essays have settings in real places—rarely are his arguments abstract, rarely are his metaphors vague and universal. But this impulse is most obvious in his fiction.

Jayber Crow begins his life in a series of dis-locations from the household, community, and even faith in God. Born within the boundaries of Port William, Jayber loses first his parents to influenza, then his adoptive parents to aging and sorrow, then his very name in the impersonal world of an orphanage (where every student is referred to by just their first initial, as in J. Crow), then his grip on God at a Bible college, then his trust in knowledge at a university. His destiny seems to be run aground on the shoals of a seedy barbershop job in a down-and-out neighborhood of Lexington, until an unmistakable call homeward—defying logic and based on no tangible remaining relationship—sets him slogging through the flooded Kentucky River valley straight to his own limit, the flood between him and Port William. But his faith is honored as Burley Coulter appears, Charon-like in his fishing skiff, to row him to the Elysium of home. That mixes the metaphors a bit, but the fact is that Jayber's journey is a religious pilgrimage, a prerational and mysterious venture propelled by a love of what once was and what might be, a hope that this place might be able to make him its own.

Once Jayber finds his niche as the town barber, he begins to learn the community's stories, and he himself becomes a character in the broad story of that place and people, so that he eventually fills the unofficial role of town historian. The barbershop affords hospitality, especially to older men who no longer have an active role except as storytellers. Though Jayber never has a family and in fact chooses to love from afar Mattie, who marries a man he deplores, he always belongs among the people and families, even after he retires to a fishing cabin outside town. His place of belonging is not found without error and misgiving, because this is a human community, fallen and fractured—but Jayber can evaluate and know his place, and others can do likewise, because he and they come to share the story and ethos of Port William, what it was, what it is, and what it might be.

Just as Berry's critique of "false hope" and diseased understandings of existence is layered, as we discussed in chapter 3, so also his constructive account of how healing communities can dwell in the world is multilayered. By putting chapter 4 between the critique and the construction, we've tried to show how the notion of finitude is not only a check and a curbing but also a baseline, a plumb line if you will, from which to build something lasting.

If we start with finitude, that boundary of human knowing and acting, then we perhaps can trace a set of creational boundaries that, when acknowledged with gratitude, allow for the construction of communities of healing. Without gratitude, one can see finitude only as oppressive, something to be trespassed, overthrown, or at least resented. But Berry reveals the life-giving nature of finitude. We suggest that he sees these boundaries in a developmental order of increasing complexity of relationships, from wilderness to land to food to body to household to community. For Berry, the lower (closer to the ground), less complex relationships make possible the higher. Our previous exploration of Berry's critique, which we laid out in chapter 3 as "order of knowing," "social order," and "order of persons," gets turned on its head to some extent here, as we highlight the doggedly concrete and embodied nature of Berry's constructive suggestions for human community. The exploration of each of these embodied layers will be the work of chapters 5 and 6.

What do we mean by layers here? These are interlaced particularities of creation, connected as life-giving structures, each and all necessary for healthy existence, each irreducible, none interchangeable. Berry's vision naturally arises from the topsoil, from the dirt under our feet, from the raw material not only of a farmer's vocation but also of human existence. In that original mingling of wild and cultivated, we begin the healing journey.

## The Wilderness beneath Our Feet

At the end of chapter 4 we focused on Berry's account of a revivified Christian response to the mystery of creation as a starting place, an essential act of humility, for the construction of healing communities. The place to start within creation, then, is at the mysterious boundary of the wilderness. Wilderness here includes real forests, real mountain ranges, real lakes and rivers and oceans. But we find that the physical connections toward which Berry points can never be reduced to purely material relationships. Though there's a vast difference between a cow and a mountain, they retain an essential connection, a mysterious affinity in their irreducibility. Also, human ordering is always bounded by mystery. Since regard for mystery gives us a humbling recognition of our place within limits, the place to start thinking about healing within creation is at the boundary of mystery, though intriguingly it is not within wilderness parks or nature preserves but in the topsoil, that we engage the mystery daily.

Though he has always been sympathetic to the work of such groups as the Sierra Club (which published his breakthrough volume *The Unsettling of America* in the mid-1970s), Berry has also been candid in his criticism of the idealistic strand of the conservation movement, because he sees a disconnect in the notion that "it is enough to save a series of islands of pristine and uninhabited wilderness in an otherwise exploited, damaged, and polluted land. And, further, that the pristine wilderness is the only alternative to exploitation and abuse."[1] The problem with such a polarization is the lack of recognition that harmony can exist in human interaction

1. "The Conservation of Nature and the Preservation of Humanity," in ATC, 71.

with creation, that cultivation can be a faithful and sustainable way to life, that God intended humans to be in creation from the start. This balancing act is not optional; it's the state we find ourselves in, and this attempt at harmony is ongoing, a constant renegotiation with the boundaries. In "Getting Along with Nature" Berry says, "humans, like all other creatures, must make a difference; otherwise, they cannot live. But unlike other creatures, humans must make a choice as to the kind and scale of the difference they make. If they choose to make too small a difference, they diminish their humanity. If they choose to make too great a difference, they diminish nature, and narrow their subsequent choices; ultimately, they diminish or destroy themselves. Nature, then, is not only our source but also our limit and measure."[2] Hence it is not by means of guilt, nor through ignorance, that we can remedy ravages and abuses; we need to fit ourselves to our world, to nurture it.

So Berry's first healing boundary is wilderness, the literal beginning (or end) of human knowing of creation. In his essay "Preserving Wildness," Berry argues that wilderness is instructive to us because its very presence reveals the limits of human control: "The reason to preserve wilderness is that we need it. We need wilderness of all kinds, large and small, public and private. We need to go now and again into places where our work is disallowed, where our hopes and plans have no standing. We need to come into the presence of the unqualified and mysterious formality of Creation."[3] Berry's statement brings out a paradox: it is not because the wilderness is chaotic and disordered that it instructs and humbles us but rather because it is ordered and formed in ways beyond our complete understanding. Wilderness teaches us by chastening our attempts to control everything around us. It is above, not beneath, our control.

What is beyond our control is still knowable, but only as a gift; it is the presence of a prior, greater order that shows us much about ourselves by limiting the scope of our activity and humbling

2. HE, 7–8.
3. Ibid., 146.

our aspirations. The life that comes every spring to a forest, or to a backyard, unaided by human cultivation, teaches us that creation works prior to our design and offers itself to be accepted on its own terms. Wilderness, in the state of not being ordered by humans, shows that another order exists. In "The Body and the Earth," Berry points out that many premodern stories emphasize the measuring of the human over against the vast creation, as a way for a human being to "recognize, finally, his true place within it, and thus be saved from both pride and from despair."[4] This measuring also allows for the human being to return as "a restorer of order, a preserver."[5] This is not a passive consciousness nor a private awakening, but an invitation to cultivate within proper scope and scale.

The healing response is then to receive the gift that allows us to recognize the wild in the cultivated, which is a way of recognizing order and limits. In "Preserving Wildness," Berry suggests that "in the recovery of culture *and* nature is the knowledge of how to farm well, how to preserve, harvest, and replenish the forests, how to make, build, and use, return and restore. In this *double* recovery, which is the recovery of our humanity, is the hope that the domestic and the wild can exist together in lasting harmony."[6]

As a gift, the wilderness is then a proper boundary from which to begin imagining the healing that will aid in this "recovering of our humanity." Berry speaks in "The Body and the Earth" of the "wilderness of Creation where we must go to be reborn—to receive the awareness, at once humbling and exhilarating, grievous and joyful, that we are a part of Creation, one with all that we live from and all that, in turn, lives from us."[7] The call to humanity from the beginning was to cultivate, and it thus put human order within the natural order, like Adam, always working the good garden in connection with a good wilderness.

4. ACP, 95.
5. Ibid.
6. HE, 142.
7. ACP, 99–100.

A caution is necessary here. When Berry says early in "Notes from an Absence and Return" that "now it is only in the wild places that a man can sense the rarity of being a man,"[8] he isn't talking about some extreme sport or Iron John "conquering" the wild and discovering oneself. This is not John Eldredge's paradigm for discovering "manly virtues." Berry has confessed to being in a "national park" sort of wilderness only a handful of times in his life. The retreat to the wild, the hermit's cave or hollow cactus, or even the rock-climbing, whitewater-rafting experience, cannot be seen as an end in itself, as health. The wilderness doesn't offer answers for bringing healing into community. It's not that we are to replace the task of human ordering with experiences of the wild; creation was never intended to be simply played in or dwelt in as a vehicle for self-discovery.

Instead, Berry's crucial recognition is the centrality of the connectedness between wild and cultivated. The fall, insofar as it places wilderness over against culture, obscures culture's rightful place, a place of work within the larger sphere of the uncontrollable, the mystery of the wilderness present everywhere. Hence, clearing and planting a garden within hedgerows and wooded boundaries can be done with humility, letting the wilderness be present. But clearcutting a forest to plant an alien crop that can be sustained only via chemical infusions can only be an act of hubris. The first can contribute to healing, the second can only be diseased.

A recognition of the wilderness's place and power in our lives leads us to ponder the place of sabbath. Sabbath, for Berry, is a recognition of the healing mystery of the rhythms and boundaries of life. Norman Wirzba's excellent account *Living the Sabbath* makes a helpful distinction between an externally imposed law (an artificial reading of sabbath) and a recognition of rhythms of creation. Wirzba underlines the necessity of attention to these rhythms: "To refuse the Sabbath is to close the world in upon ourselves, by making it yield to our desires and designs, and to cut ourselves off from God's presence and purpose."[9] So it is right to come to wilderness

---

8. GGL, 41.
9. Norman Wirzba, *Living the Sabbath* (Grand Rapids: Brazos, 2006), 34.

for sabbath; though it is not to be our dwelling place, we can't live without it.

A privileging of either wilderness or culture is a path of mistaking disease for healing—either we abandon our task and connection as cultivators for some ephemeral "return to nature" or we act in hubris toward wilderness, conquering rather than cultivating. For Berry, experience has shown that as the human footprint exceeds sustainable proportion, both wilderness *and* culture suffer. Furthermore, there's no clear formula for identifying and fostering the balance between wilderness and culture, though awareness of the creational rhythms of work and rest, of control and "letting be," nurtures within us a sensitivity toward wholeness and connection. Wilderness, as a kind of sabbath, shows us how to relinquish control—a key notion of creatureliness.

## The Soil and the Land

The boundary of wilderness is not a static line between field and woods. The relationship is more dynamic, because the soil itself that we live upon and cultivate always retains a measure of wildness. Soil is a very recognizable boundary, always somewhere beneath our feet (though asphalt, concrete, and landscaper's sod all inhibit our awareness; as Hopkins lamented in "God's Grandeur," "Nor can foot feel, being shod"). Yet both the land we live on and the soil we work with retain their mystery, their natural order, which we ignore only at our peril. As children of Adam (whose name means "dirt"), we are inextricably connected to the soil, and we are further called to interact with the earth as cultivators, though after the curse the mystery of this relationship is accompanied with tension. The soil is the medium of life, the link between the wild and the cultivated. Indeed, life is lived *in media*, somewhere between the miracle of life and the work that produces the tangible fruits in hand. Berry points out in "Preserving Wildness" that "the topsoil, to the extent that it is fertile, is wild; it is a dark wilderness, ultimately unknowable, teeming with wildlife."[10] Elsewhere Berry notes that a proper connection to the soil is best captured by the notion of husbandry: "What is husbanded is ultimately a mystery. A farmer, as one of his farmer correspondents once wrote to Liberty Hyde Bailey, is 'a dispenser of the 'Mysteries of God.' "[11]

The soil is the place where we engage the wilderness by means of cultivation, not to destroy or tame it but to nurture it, to allow it to nourish us. This is the creational role of the earth and the creational task of humanity. The literal cultivation of the land is a starting point for the analogy of culture, just as it is a threshold between knowing and mystery. In "The Gift of the Good Land," Berry states, "The Creator's love for the Creation is mysterious precisely because it does not conform to human purposes."[12] Hence, cultivation is not ownership or control; we note again that Berry prefers the term *usufruct*, which connotes the limited but meaningful role we have stewarding that which has been given to us as a gift.

There is no human flourishing that is not literally "grounded," yet one of Berry's most persistent laments is the detachment of humanity from the soil, specifically through reductionistic forces of progress, borrowed from industry to inform agriculture. In his essay "Renewing Husbandry," Berry reflects upon two different ways of approaching the soil: " 'Soil science,' as practiced by soil scientists, and even more as it has been handed down to farmers, has tended to treat the soil as a lifeless matrix in which 'soil chemistry' takes place and 'nutrients' are 'made available.' And this, in turn, has made farming increasingly shallow—literally so—in its understanding of the soil. The modern farm is understood as a surface on which various mechanical operations are performed, and to which various chemicals are applied. The under-surface of reality of organisms and roots in mostly ignored."[13] As a counterpoint, Berry offers one of his revivified terms: " 'Soil husbandry' is a different kind of study,

10. HE, 140.
11. "Renewing Husbandry," in WI, 98–99; Liberty Hyde Bailey was a distinguished professor in the School of Agriculture at Cornell University in the early twentieth century.
12. ACP, 298.
13. WI, 98.

involving a different kind of mind. Soil husbandry leads, in the words of Sir Albert Howard, to understanding 'health in soil, plant, animal, and man as one great subject.' We apply the word 'health' only to living creatures, and to soil husbandry a healthy soil is a wilderness, mostly unstudied and unknown, but teemingly alive. The soil is at once a living community of creatures and their habitat. The farm's husband, its family, its crop and animals, all are members of the soil community; all belong to the character and identity of the place."[14] In my role as a small farmer / large gardener, I (Matt) have learned to reckon with the sandy, acidic soil of west Michigan, which dries out quickly and needs to be constantly nourished to build up humus. I (Michael), in my city garden some twenty-five miles to the south, deal with a clayey soil, water drainage issues, and a variety of citified rodents. Neither of us can simply go to a big-box store to buy some universal formula for standardizing the soil, but this has not stopped the lawn-care services of the world from attempting to green our grasses (and our streams and rivers) by means of "mechanical operations" and "chemicals."

Berry asserts, in "Agriculture from the Roots Up," that "harmony between our human economy and the natural world—local adaptation—is a perfection that we will never finally achieve, but must continuously try for."[15] Here the task of finding the proper direction for our activity is linked strongly to the temporal nature of our existence; a static solution will not do, but we are called to nurture the earth at the most basic level.

This notion of "the land as the gift given" harks back to our discussion of the structure of creation. Structure is a given that is beyond human control and manipulation but is accessible through a faithful response to the call. So, then, Berry's analysis of the use and misuse of

14. Ibid. In another essay from the same volume, "Agriculture from the Roots Up," Berry notes that the Land Institute of Kansas, guided by his long-time friend Wes Jackson, is a tangible defender of the soil but also a spiritual force responding to a "war against nature [that] destroys the health of our water and soil." A "roots up" agriculture promotes the culture of life over the culture of death precisely because it operates in harmony with creation and "exposes also the weakness of industrial economy" (109).

15. WI, 111.

land is exemplary of our understanding of directional choices within creation, aiming toward life or toward death. For Berry, it is foolhardy to try to address the diseases of culture without acknowledging the crucial role of the wilderness, of the dirt, for healing.

Berry lists several questions that are essential to ask about the soil's health, and they resonate with analogies to human social health, among them "Is our health in any way separable from the health of our economic landscape?"[16] He then avers, "If we cannot establish an enduring or even a humanly bearable economy by our attempt to defeat nature, then we will have to try living in harmony and co-operation with her."[17] To ask these questions is to develop a kind of "science of place" that shows the connections and the boundaries—a "place-ology" that is ultimately the science of health.

In "Native Grasses and What They Mean," Berry judges the older farming methods to edify beyond mere utility: "It was a native farming method at once skillful, thrifty, respectful of the land, and saving of it. To describe its complexity and intelligence, its wakeful determination to preserve the field while using it, one can only say it was elegant."[18] He offers similar aesthetic language regarding his visit to a familial set of Amish farms, recounted in "Elmer Lapp's Place," when he suggests that clarity of place is an end in itself: "All the patterns of the farm are finally gathered into an ecological pattern; it is one 'household,' its various parts joined to each other and the whole joined to nature, to the world, by liking, by delighted and affectionate understanding. The ecological pattern is a pattern of pleasure."[19] In such a household, he says in "People, Land, and Community," "people are joined to the land by work," a relation-ship distinct in every way from the "harried labor of industrial economy." When work is done in improper ways and proportions, however, it becomes exploitation, and so "we have exchanged har-mony for an interminable fuss, and the work of culture for the time

16. Ibid., 109.
17. Ibid.
18. GGL, 86.
19. Ibid., 226.

and harried labor of an industrial economy."[20] In the late 1960s, reflecting on his connection to his farm in "Notes from an Absence and Return," Berry lamented the curious disconnections that were already pervading our culture: "All these places of unforced loveliness, whose details keep touching in my mind the memory of great paintings, now lie within the sound of the approach of an alien army whose bulldozers fly the flag of the American economy (hardly the economy of the topsoil). This country is an unknown place suffering the invasion of a people whose minds have never touched the earth."[21]

So how can we come to know the soil, as a way of knowing ourselves and each other? One way might be to take the task literally: Steve Bouma-Prediger suggested in a guest lecture in a class we taught together that students might make themselves more "at home" by learning the species of every tree on the campus (no easy task, even with our limited tree population!).

One of the intriguing angles that Berry offers on this essential connection of land to person comes in his critique of the slave economy of his forebears in his work *The Hidden Wound*. The connection of the land with such human wrong suddenly raises the stakes on the costs of dislocating:

> The white race in America has marketed and destroyed more of the fertility of the earth in less time than any other race that ever lived. In my part of the country, at least, this is largely to be accounted for by the racial division of the *experience* of the landscape. The white man, preoccupied with the abstractions of the economic exploitation and ownership of the land, necessarily has lived on the country as a destructive force, an ecological catastrophe, because he assigned the hand labor, and in that the possibility of intimate knowledge of the land, to a people he considered racially inferior; in thus debasing labor, he destroyed the possibility of a meaningful contact with the earth.[22]

20. ACP, 189.
21. CH, 46–7.
22. HW, 105.

This account that Berry offers is an historical angle regarding the nineteenth century, but it is also relevant to the agricultural practices that evolved in America in the twentieth century. The agricultural industry's pervasive use of migrant workers has kept alive the economic, racial, and social divisions between those who own the land and those who work the land. Our demand for cheap food has necessitated efficiencies that separate us from the soil and place the burden on the backs of the lower class that does the work.

Our ability to buy attractive produce in an air-conditioned super-market-temple of food, at a low price, any time of the year, is based upon a deception. The low price is not necessarily based on more efficient production but on our willingness to care only about the end and to push the means—people, land, and the delicate relationship of cultivation—as far from ourselves as possible. Our willingness to live with this deception leads to the ridiculous nature of the ag-ricultural market—recall the Michigan juice company's decision to import its apple juice concentrate from China, because the margins were slightly lower than they would be if working with the multitu-dinous orchards all around it. And by reiterating such an example, we've shifted to another layer where healing is needed—the realm of the fruit of the earth, our food. Let's look now at the surprising role of food in our difficult directional choices.

## You Are What You Eat

The production, distribution, and consumption of food reveal our basic fidelities and allegiances. No human being is divorced from this basic relationship. "How" and the "how much" are the knotted questions behind the "what" of diet. In his introduction to *The Art of the Commonplace*, Norman Wirzba tells us, "We must learn to resist those practices that further isolate us and turn us away from the earth. This can begin practically by cultivating a new relationship with food. Food, rather than being simply fuel, is the most concrete and intimate connection between ourselves and the earth that exists."[23] Berry himself notes, "The real problem of food production occurs within the complex, mutually influential relationship of soil, plants, animals and people."[24] Our society's preferred means of food production trespass the boundary here in manifold ways. The first stage might be a monoculture farm, abandoning the diversification that helps maintain human beings' close connection to earth and food and simply growing things for some other person or entity. Further along, the removal of any human connection to the land and to food production eliminates healthy boundaries by at once narrowing the scope—such that food comes from the "nowhere" of the supermarket shelf—and expanding unhealthily, as we demand limitless access to all sorts of foods throughout the year. And this is the real danger, this demand for limits to be obliterated, because such an urge will likely not stop with grocery shopping but grow into a lifestyle.

One sign of disease is to see food only as a consumer good that mysteriously appears in the supermarket, such that health is quantified in terms of the number of selections and breadth of choices available year round, regardless of origin and transportation costs. In the diseased approach, "food is pretty much an abstract idea, until it appears on the grocery shelf or on the table."[25] This reduction is as severe as in any sphere of human existence: "The passive American consumer, sitting down to a meal of pre-prepared or fast food, confronts a platter covered with inert, anonymous substances that have been processed, dyed, breaded, sauced, gravied, ground, pulped, strained, blended, prettified, and sanitized beyond resemblance to any part of any creature that ever lived. The products of nature and agriculture have been made, to all appearances, the products of industry. Both eater and eaten are thus in exile from biological reality,"[26] trapped within and deceived by "the ideal of industrialism, a walled city surrounded by valves that let merchandise

23. ACP, xviii.
24. "Solving for Pattern," in ACP, 269.
25. "Pleasures of Eating," ACP, 322.
26. Ibid., 323.

in, but no consciousness out."[27] When food is understood primarily as consumer product, then, the disease manifests itself.

Berry suggests a very basic reestablishment of healthy connection to food and land: "I begin with the proposition that eating is an agricultural act."[28] He argues further that "one reason to eat responsibly is to live free."[29] It is within limits and self-discipline that we find freedom, as we recognize and respect creational boundaries. Berry's goal is to turn around the condescension of humans toward food, to reckon with our humbleness and need. In his poem "Prayer after Eating," Berry articulates this hopeful vision toward food:

> I have taken in the light
> that quickened eye and leaf.
> May my brain be bright with praise
> of what I eat, in the brief blaze
> of motion and of thought.
> May I be worthy of my meat.[30]

Such reverential language is also present in his wonderful poem "The Satisfactions of the Mad Farmer," with its litany of "raspberries ripe and heavy amid their foliage, / currants shining red in clusters amid their foliage, / strawberries red ripe with the white / flowers still on the vines—picked / with the dew on them, before breakfast . . ."[31] This is a kind of liturgy of fruitfulness, in which each of the earth's fruits merits a moment of awed contemplation.

It is not only in Berry's poems that food takes on a religious, ceremonial nature; in his fiction, meals are often, if not Eucharistic, certainly befitting the *agape* feast. In *The Memory of Old Jack*, the noonday meal for the tobacco harvesters has this quality, with the octogenarian Jack presiding as elder and officiant. In *Jayber Crow*, the catfish meal that Burley and his mother prepare

27. Ibid., 324.
28. Ibid., 321.
29. Ibid., 323.
30. SP, 83.
31. CP, 133.

for Jayber, as a sort of rite of acceptance after his three days of wandering in the rain, has the feel of the shore of Galilee with fish and honeycomb. Tentatively, fostered by hospitality and the concrete reality of food being eaten, a sort of resurrection of Jayber back into his rightful place begins. These are just some of the hints and guesses at what intimate connection between food and person can mean.

# 6

.............

# Bodies, Households, Communities

## Health within Finitude

### Connecting Body with Soul

A conversation about the "body" is an apt extension of our "from the ground up" tracing of wilderness, soil, and food. That our bodies are "from the ground" is a basic creational truth,[1] and that the body is wild before it is cultured is a foundational notion for Berry. Bodily appetites are present in the natural order in a way that makes possible, but does not assume, the work of the cultural order. Only as embodied persons can we engage in culture-making—culture is not a purely spiritual task, nor can a life-giving culture simply grow from the appetites.

Berry finds it dangerous that mere repression of appetite can be seen as healthy. "You cannot devalue the body and value the soul—or value anything else,"[2] he writes in "The Body and the Earth." He sees that "the isolation of the body sets it in direct conflict with ev-

---

1. Genesis 2:7: "out of the dust of the ground . . ."
2. ACP, 100.

erything else in Creation."[3] Unlike much Christian discourse opposing Gnostic tendencies that divide the body and soul, critiques that are mainly couched in abstract spiritual language, Berry's analysis begins with the body as the positive foundation for image bearers in communion with the Creator and with each other. Because of their intrinsic value, given by God, neither the soil nor the body needs justification. However, both require cultivation if they are to give life. Uncultivated soil has only limited fruitfulness; the wild apple tree gives apples, but they are sporadic, vulnerable fruit. Likewise, a human body's directionless responses to appetite may yield some fruit of pleasure, but it is often bitter and highly vulnerable.

These destructive possibilities correlate to the recurring danger we've been tracking—a lack of respect for mystery and boundary and an attendant urge to take control, in this case of our appetites. As the farmer cultivates the wild soil to bring forth life, embodied in food and fodder, so also we cultivate our bodies to become more human. The twin errors are present and possible again: one can leave the body an uncultivated wilderness, a chaos of immediate impulses and easy pleasures, unmoderated by any genuine discipline. Or one can overcompensate, overcultivate, to the point of hatred of the body, of strict constraints on bodily realities. Today's rejection of wilderness often involves a rejection of embodiment that is not so much ascetic as cosmetic. We have many more fitness centers, plastic surgeons, and Botox clinics in our suburbs than we do monasteries or flagellants on our street corners. The impulse to control is thus a manipulation that will play right up close to the sort of qualifications for the immoderate, appetitive life that we are loath to surrender: sex appeal is the result of our contemporary self-abnegation.

This misdirection is particularly ironic in its end result: "And it is clear to anyone who looks carefully at any crowd that we are wasting our bodies exactly as we are wasting our land. Our bodies are fat, weak, joyless, sickly, ugly, the virtual prey of the manufacturers of medicine and cosmetics. Our bodies have become marginal; they are

3. Ibid.

104

growing useless like our 'marginal' land because we have less and less use for them."[4]

Since to be human is to live within limits of grief and joy, to be at home with our finite embodiment, we must see our bodies as the creational gift that guides all our connections in the world. When modernity fails to recognize as authoritative our corporeal limits, thus treating our finitude as a flaw, the only result can be a restlessness and constant striving against ourselves. We have already referred to Berry's idea that "healing is impossible in loneliness. . . . Conviviality is healing."[5] We must reckon with the body's centrality, as the medium in which we dwell, *and* its finitude, as we are drawn to relationships. A body is particular, but in recognizing that particularity we also recognize that we can find our way into the world only through relationships, both with the earth (food, climate, etc.) and with other creatures, especially other people. Our identity is given—we are not self-constructions. As recipients of God's gift of our particular selfhood, we have limits and boundaries that are not of our choosing. And insofar as limits create both the need and the possibility of connection, so also our relationships, body to body and self to self, are given.

Failure to recognize these limits places us in peril. "Contempt for the body is invariably manifested in contempt for other bodies—the bodies of slaves, laborers, women, animals, plants, the earth itself. Relationships with all other creatures become competitive and exploitive rather than collaborative and convivial. The world is seen and dealt with, not as an ecological community, but as a stock exchange, the ethics of which are based on the tragically misnamed 'law of the jungle.' This 'jungle' law is a basic fallacy of modern culture."[6] That fallacy is expressed in the modern nightclub, which appears to be teeming with life, sound, movement, a multiplicity of individualized bodies. But the possibility of relationship is reduced to conquest. Even the most stylized appetites, whether imaged in *Sex in the City* or in *Desperate Housewives*, are uncultured and weedy when looked at from this perspective.

4. Ibid., 103.
5. Ibid., 99.
6. Ibid., 101.

## Uncultivated Sexuality

This sexual distortion is not the only example—others include our abuses of food and our proclivity to physical violence—but the sexual seems to have inexorable force in our culture. Yet the notion of an autonomous sexual identity, which we could carry around like a debit card or currency of exchange, is undermined by the communal nature of everyone's very embodiment. Embodiment, in Berry's sense, is not expressed in mere surrender to appetites, because such a route destroys the "other." To be uncultured is to be destructive, and this always extends beyond the individual. The sexual distortion of embodiment fosters the seeking of boundless pleasure which abuses the limits between each other and between self and community. But Berry's diagnosis is not rooted in fearfulness or flight from our own sexuality. In fact, he is surprisingly hopeful about the very sexual instincts that have so confounded our culture.

Berry is careful to give place to our sexual selves (as we all must), arguing that "the instinctive sexuality within which marriage exists must somehow be made to thrive within marriage. To divide one from the other is to degrade both, and ultimately to destroy marriage. . . . And marriage must recognize that it survives because of, as well as in spite of, Kalypso and Paris, and the generosity of instinct that they represent. It must give some ceremonially acknowledged place to the sexual energies that now thrive outside all established forms in the destructive freedom of moral ignorance or disregard."[7] Rather than fleeing from the body's instincts, we need to properly place them. We needn't shut down the nightclub, but we need to reinvent within its walls a context akin to the communal dances of, say, Jane Austen's novels, where sexual energy can find place in rituals of communal celebration and courtship. Sexual instinct must be cultivated, ordered, and allowed to bring life.

In case we haven't noted this before, once or a dozen times, this transition will be a tall order for our contemporary culture—it's

7. Ibid., 125.

not merely the dance floor, the place of public interaction, that is implicated but the very images and symbols of our discourse. Berry notes in "Sex, Economy, Freedom, Community" that the body is commodified and debased by contemporary advertising, and "where the body has no dignity, where the sanctity of its own mystery and privacy is not recognized by a surrounding and protecting community, there can be no freedom."[8] In spite of its ubiquity, uncultivated sexuality is treated as only an issue of individual desire. At its core, this is the problem—the seeming path to freedom is a path to enslavement. So sexuality cannot remain a private, individual issue in Berry's estimation; the notion of private moral commitments that undergirds all contemporary discourse on sexuality is reductionistic. It is also a fragmented way to try and see ourselves, separating sexual energy from household and community. Thus, rather than being healing and life-giving, sexual energy actually threatens the life of both: "When it's no longer allied by proximity and analogy to the nurturing disciplines that bound the household to the cycles of fertility and the seasons, life and death, then sexual love loses its symbolic or ritualistic force, its deepest solemnity and its highest joy. It loses its sense of consequence and responsibility."[9] Among the obvious dissolutions of family and kinship, Berry calls out the double violence against self and other of abortion, perhaps the most heinous of the consequences.

## Bounded Appetites: The Work of Marriage

> Marriages to marriages
> are joined, husband and wife
> are plighted to all
> husbands and wives,
> any life has all lives
> for its delight.[10]

8. SEFC, 166–67.
9. ACP, 112.
10. "In Rain," in CP, 268.

Our vision of marriage and household has been warped by sophisticated but uncultured views of sexuality. What energizes that vision, says Berry, is the lure of "sexual romance . . . the sentimentalization of sexual love that for generations has been the work of popular songs and stories."[11] Among the falsehoods stemming from this is the healthy-sounding claim that "monogamous marriage is therefore logical and natural, and forsaking all others involves no difficulty."[12] This disregards the point that Berry has argued, that our sexuality needs disciplining to stay within the particularity of a place. When a young couple is told that marriage is easy and blissful, an isolated endeavor between just the two of them, the potential for disillusionment and disease is heightened, along with the possibility that their sexual energy will remain disordered and undisciplined. Uncultivated wilderness is always a threat: by it "the energy that is the most convivial and unifying loses its communal forms and becomes divisive."[13]

Thinking about "cultivation" from natural order to human order thus leads our discussion of sexuality directly into a discussion of marriage and household. Lauren Winner has outlined this connection well in her book *Real Sex*, especially in her chapter "Communal Sex, Or, Why Your Neighbor Has Any Business Asking You What You Did Last Night." As she outlines the code of privacy that many friends uphold with one another with reference to their sex lives, Winner is drawn to Berry's countercultural analysis:

A robust yet judicious understanding of the communal nature of sexual behavior requires that Christians enact both a thicker understanding of sex and a thicker understanding of community. To return sex to its proper place within creation, to revivify a gracious and salutary sexual existence, we need to root out the modern and hyperindividualistic notions about sex, and come to understand the place of sex in the Christian—and human—community. . . . Enter Wendell Berry, who suggests that marital sex ought not to be an

11. ACP, 112.
12. Ibid., 113.
13. Ibid.

108

individual project at all. In a rich domestic context, sex is not about individual desires that happen to be neatly matched, but is rather an embodied way of entering into community with one's spouse and of enacting God's love.[14]

For Berry, marriage represents not merely the cultivation of sexual instinct but also an establishment of household, which is a kind of community. As Winner points out, "*Household* seems, at first blush, to be synonymous for *home*, but it is actually quite different from what most of us mean when we speak of home."[15] She traces Berry's argument to its historical antecedents: "Think back to the eighteenth century when people did most of their productive labor together, in family units, in their households. . . . Your household was not a place where individuals happened to congregate; it was a place of genuine mutuality."[16]

It is in the mutuality of marriage that sexuality becomes properly public, since, in Winner's words, "Berry wants us to envision domestic life and sex, marriage and the marriage bed, as 'a more generous enclosure—a household welcoming to neighbors and friends.'"[17] Within the act of marriage, proper boundaries are placed not only upon the husband and wife but upon all members of the community. Rather than being exclusive and private, it is inclusive and public. Once these proper limits are recognized, healthy marriages, households, and communities evolve simultaneously, since marriages and communities are encultured in analogous ways. The couple's identity is given by the community and to the community; the couple's story becomes a patch in the quilt.

Despite the rhetorical power of this talk of public sexuality, Berry is quite aware that there is a whole other publicizing of sexuality that is deadly. At the inevitable risk of dating ourselves, the movie *Pretty Woman* leaps to mind as an archetype for this blighted notion

14. Lauren Winner, *Real Sex: The Naked Truth about Chastity* (Grand Rapids: Brazos, 2005), 54–55.
15. Ibid., 55.
16. Ibid., 56.
17. Ibid, 57.

of public sexuality as romantic vehicle, rootless but overpowering. Berry argues clearly in "Sex, Economy, Freedom, Community" that public displays of sexual intimacy—whether in film or in advertising—are exploitive, because the "intimacy, the union itself, remains unobserved." Once the intimacy is removed, the purposes are lost: "The essential and inscrutable privacy of sexual love is the sign, both of its mystery and sanctity, and of its humorousness."[18] The household provides the proper context where intimacy is practiced and nurtured, and in so doing, the household itself is given proper order. Marriage is an act that creates one kind of household, which, alongside faith community and political community (and others), is a normative embodiment of community. Marriage is a kind of microcosmic community, with anticipations in the household of larger dynamics.

The key role of household has led to Berry's intriguing notion of "home economics." In the preface to his 1987 volume of essays by that name, he muses, "My title is borrowed from a school course, and I do not intend it entirely in fun. Its redundancy seems to acknowledge that what passes now for economics, like what passes now for national defense, has strayed far from any idea of home, either the world or the world's natural ecosystems and human households."[19] This is a unique middle territory that Berry is mapping out. Household is the bridge between individual and community, the place where character is cultivated, where work is done both for sustenance and for the formation of virtue. This is also a middle ground for reflection on more integral embodiments, but reflection that does not require the abstraction of a science. Here reflection is always embodied and practiced in a concrete way, though by no means insular; one's household makes sense only within the context of the many households that surround it and the concerns of each and every. The home economy is not a measure of income and purchasing power and is certainly not something that can be outsourced through external employment. It is more about fidelity and hospitality and

18. ACP, 175.
19. HE, x.

110

frugality (which is in turn about nurturing rather than penurious budgeting). There is no template for how to create a household, no methodology or menu that will fit every family. Still, in the case of a central function, such as mealtime, selecting and preparing and sharing food need to be carried out in a disciplined fashion. At the same time, if nutrition for your family, or quantity, or even localness of your food source becomes the dominant ideology to the detriment of a healthy, hospitable place of meeting and eating, then the practice of household has not yet been achieved. Practices have to have a purpose, and so home economics is pointing to an end of disciplined choices that connect the members of the household both to creation and to community.

The public nature of marriage, as Berry casts it, is thus extended and deepened by the pursuit of a deliberate home economics. In Berry's novella *Andy Catlett: Early Travels*, we glimpse in the two sets of grandparents two different, but equally valid, formulations of home economics. With the rural Catlett grandparents, the tempo of life is slower, as they are not yet accelerated by electricity or automobiles, and are still anchored in a simple pattern of work and meals and rest. It is a home economics of frugality; they have sent two sons to college (and one, Andy's dad Wheeler, to law school). In Port William, the small town nearby, Andy's "town" grandparents, the Feltners, have their farm right off the main street and live by what we might call a more "cosmopolitan" rhythm. They have a jalopy, indoor plumbing, and they are involved in some of the town's civic institutions (Mat Feltner is on the bank board)—their table often includes extended family and acquaintances. Yet, in both households, a place is kept for Andy, a literal place at the table, a place as recipient of the various stories that make up the families' intertwined histories. And that place continues to be kept no matter what Andy does or where he goes, as long as the grandparents live; ultimately, it is not Andy's place to take but what has been given to him. He is part of their households and therefore is shaped by their various disciplines and connected to their communal lives.

111

Later in his own journey, when he has left home to work as a journalist and pursue a career, Andy will find out how difficult it is to sustain a household once he has disconnected from the place and people who shaped him. In trying to "make his place in the world," he finds himself placeless.[20] Though Andy eventually comes back home and reestablishes his place in Port William and among his people by redeeming a dying farm, he is the exception in Port William (and most of the United States) in the decades following World War II. Transience becomes the social norm, and many of the grandchildren of the Catletts and Feltners end up moving to bigger cities, disappearing from the rolls of Port William and leaving few or no strings attached. The novels *Jayber Crow* and *Hannah Coulter* depict this same slow fragmentation, detachment, and ultimately displacement, which Berry has also lamented in his poetry and essays.

One of Berry's persistent insights is that healthy households cannot be fostered when work is utterly external to the home. When our work is nothing more than a resented imposition from which we attempt to escape, our home becomes merely a place of recreation. Berry calls for a return of work to the home, because this is the place where character and communal virtues are formed. Rather than a place of escape, it can be a place of authentic work—marriage work, parenting work, stewarding together the family's resources. In the 1980 essay "Family Work," Berry argues that "we also know that growing and preparing food at home can provide family work—work for everybody. And by thus elaborating household chores and obligations, we hope to strengthen the bonds of interest, loyalty, affection, and cooperation that keep families together."[21] Neither idyllic nor easy, such a context for work seems nevertheless to restore a consistency of aim and purpose to this realm of increasing fragmentation. As parents ourselves, we can see a possible angst in reading Berry as tacitly demanding a return to the agrarian world of obvious shared work, with the daily chores of farm and hearth determining the rhythm of a child's life. Most of us will not quit

20. See especially the novel *Remembering*.
21. GGL, 155.

our jobs outside the home, but all of us can thoughtfully foster a home economics where everyone in the household feels included in a common task, a common shaping of character, a common set of practices. In short, only in the practice of a home economics does a house become a home.

If life doesn't appear to be filled with enough tasks—after all, everything from dishwashing to yard care is highly automated—then honoring limits and boundaries will likely bring with it more labor. Picking, washing, sorting, and preparing locally grown produce takes more time and effort than microwaving a bag of frozen peas. Pulling up weeds together in a sidewalk or garden or front lawn is more time consuming than wielding a bottle of weed killer. Walking to church or to a shop or library is more tiring and time-intensive than piling in the van to zip across town. But such tasks, such actual efforts to use our own renewable energy, done together with an eye toward both creation and community, can form the basis of solid home economics.

Though this vision has been damaged by modernity, Lauren Winner provides a hopeful account of how a reweaving of such a fabric might begin. Using the trope of the backyard neighborly barbecue, she shows that "you don't have to be an eighteenth-century farmer to begin to conceive of your home as a household. Rather, beginning to approach your meals, chores, and furnishings as part of a rich domestic economy, opportunities to connect you, your family, and your neighbors in truly shared undertakings."[22]

## Healing Communities

We all know that households are not utopias, nor are the local communities that they ideally help to build. Still, when a household is based upon proper ordering of sexuality and of work, its members are able to reach out and interact in community, as order begets order. Just as we order and nurture soil to grow plants, so also we

22. Winner, *Real Sex*, 56.

113

must order and nurture the growth of human relationships. But home economics is not quite Berry's end. Instead, he points to the community, local in scope, both fragile and enduring, as the natural boundary whereby one is still in a place.

Communities are the ways in which households open up and become invitational to each other. Healthy communities maintain an invitational role toward other communities, both near and far, but this cannot be reduced to an economic, parasitical set of relationships. Healthy communities can recognize connections to all humans, to the earth, to the soil, to plants and weather and sun and moon, yet also remain particular to a place and a set of people. The land on which the households dwell is irreducible in its particularity. Berry has argued in "Sex, Economy, Freedom, Community" that "a healthy community is like an ecosystem, and it includes—or it makes itself harmoniously a part of—its local ecosystem. It is also like a household; it is the household of its place, and it includes the households of many families, human and nonhuman. And to extend Saint Paul's famous metaphor by only a little, a healthy community is like a body, for its members mutually support and serve one another."[23] It is consciously vulnerable, living between grief and joy, comfortable with death and limit, comfortable with brevity and mortality.

What it refuses to be comfortable with is a self-imposed disease and death that promises life as quantity and boundless potential. If we keep reinventing the self in isolation from its locale, we perpetuate mass isolation under the guise of trends and popular theories. When placeless corporations replace local businesses, when Hollywood replaces local stories, when absentee landlords replace local ownership, this disfigurement of community is enacted.

Much of the time we work with inadequate understandings of community: dislocation is addressed purely as a spatial problem, and proximity is given as the cure for "human distance." Healthy communities are moored in particular households, which by their very nature protect against abstraction, by providing the only place

23. SEFC, 155.

where hospitality—the acceptance of the "other" as embodied—can take place. This protects us from both a radical individualism and an idealized public world devoid of particularities. These poles will be addressed in chapter 7.

For now, we assert with Berry that a healing community must be placed. Indeed, the problem of community cannot even be addressed beyond a certain scope and scale, and when the conversation is abstracted toward the idealized "public," it ceases to be about what Berry understands as community. He further argues in "Sex, Economy, Freedom, Community" that the overarching value given to "pluralism" in our society is a deceptive abstraction, beginning with the "who" questions and ignoring the "where" question that is central for Berry. His claim that "there are only pluralities of local cultures,"[24] rather than narrowing the conversation away from pluralism into a myopic rural American idealism, vivifies the accounting of the diversity of our culture. What Berry wants is to see each particular community in a particular place, to recognize difference without division, to shun the easy abstractions and sweeping generalities that explain everything and yet nothing about our nation's communities. The fact that you can be plopped down on the "main strip" of any American town and be faced with the exact same set of retail and consumption variables is in itself an abstracting of our lives that cannot be communal.

Berry's constructive account of our gifts and callings, from wilderness all the way to community, is one of the most insightful readings we've ever encountered as to how human culture can remain healthy. Here, though, we'd like to open and investigate the notion of community a bit further, not to tweak Berry's ideas so much as to pursue a few paths he's opened for us. We recognize that different types of communities must negotiate their identities differently with one another: whereas Berry casts the local community as the primary unit, to which all others are subordinate, we would suggest that multiple layers of human order—faith, economic, political—all play a role

24. Ibid., 171.

115

in the shaped community. For Berry, location is *the* crucial element, whereas we suggest that it is *a* crucial element but that identity is also shaped by religious influences, economics, and political forces. Berry does recognize these layers, but he underplays their significance. Where Berry might see community as a wagon wheel, with locality as its hub, we'd shift the image to a spider web wherein locality is one strand interwoven among the many others, or (to further the metaphorical shifts) we would bring forward the patchwork quilt that we suggested before. The quilt image is helpful because every element of the community is significant and unique, yet each must be subordinate to the whole pattern that gives the quilt, and hence the community, its healthy identity.

Further, some virtues carry through the whole continuum of different layers/patches/strands of community. For example, trust and hospitality run through every set of relationships, but a family is not a classroom is not a polling booth—the manifestations will be different, though the ordering principle should remain constant. Meanwhile there are other sorts of virtues that must be seen as particular to a certain layer, in order to keep healthy boundaries. So the virtue of piety, particularly in terms of reverence and worship, is apt for the religious layer but would be inappropriate if lauded as the highest virtue in either the educational or the political layer. In Berry's fiction, the universe of Port William has a dynamic quality, but it is mostly a social sphere that bears the notion of "membership"; the church, the school, and commerce in general are left at the fringe. Hence issues of piety and inquiry and justice are underdeveloped in Berry's work. Lauren Winner made a shrewd observation along these lines during a conversation in one of our classes in the spring of 2007. She raised the question of the status of women and the quality of life offered them historically by rural communities. Does the boundary of the household become too much an enclosure? How might women participate fully in community life? These sorts of questions, as Winner pointed out, don't receive clear answers in Berry's fiction. One might also ask, how do marginalized groups of all sorts fit into Berry's notion of local, healing community? Without trying to sweep away these good questions, we'd make a start by pointing out that, in Berry's work, the social virtues of hospitality, frugality, and gratitude are ubiquitous and almost always movingly rendered.

Even in the limited scope of his insight into community, Berry's general notion that there are no abstract communities is still tremendously revealing, because he diagnoses the disease of placelessness with an uncompromising strength. His message, though not systematic, is nevertheless a clarion call for us to foster healthy communities.

For Berry the bounded community is the unavoidable context out of which to talk about lived existence, and his expositions set an invaluable groundwork for a renewed understanding. He leaves us all to navigate what the living out of community will look like in each idiosyncratic, placed, and particular community. Given his distrust of formulaic answers, one can understand Berry's persistent distrust of movements, which he sees as promulgating nothing more than abstract prescriptions. Whether we like it or not, we must be vigilant to figure out the best embodiments of community in this place, in this time, among these people, in this creation. To borrow Berry's trope and to change it a bit, a community is not only "the household of a place" but it is always a "community of communities," with the layers never cleanly separated nor isolated from one another.

The rhetoric of our world, of nation-state and global village, seems at odds with this formulation. Hence, we need to consider why health must start within the local community. Doesn't such an idea seem parochial and backward in the dynamism of contemporary cultural expansion? But Berry is uncompromising on this point; whenever he addresses the issue of community, his primary goal is to keep the focus within the bounded circle. He reminds us that the discourse on what is good and right has always flourished within the context of a given community. What sense does "Love your neighbor" make if you never know your neighbors? Health means connection for Berry, and the most important connection is face to face, embodied person to embodied person.

But the triumph of industrialization has changed the focus, shifted it from the particular to the massive, the small to the large: "The message is plain enough, and we have ignored it for too long: the great, centralized economic entities of our time do not come into rural places in order to improve them by 'creating jobs.' They come to take as much of value as they can take, as cheaply and as quickly as they can take it. . . . They are not interested in the good health—economic or natural or human—of any place on this earth. . . . The ideal of the modern corporation is to be (in terms of its own advantage) anywhere and (in terms of local accountability) nowhere."[25] How do we recover a "somewhere" in the midst of this "nowhere" culture? How do we ground our decisions within our lived existence, instead of in the abstract methodology of experts and politicians? Berry suggests it is precisely our web of relationships, bounded in local community, that can offer us each a healthy context: "But our decisions can also be informed—our loves both limited and strengthened—by those patterns of value and restraint, principle and expectation, memory, familiarity and understanding that, inwardly, add up to *character* and outwardly to culture."[26] Thus, in Berry's vision of community, a powerful dialogical interplay occurs as characters forge culture together, culture that then helps shape each particular character. In the "membership of Port William" that populates Berry's fiction, it would be inappropriate to attempt a characterization of any particular figure apart from his or her link to the broader community. One could never understand the pattern of a quilt by looking at a single patch, nor does the patch have its fullness apart from the broader pattern. One small example: the significance of Jarratt Coulter, an old, taciturn farmer-uncle who is a rather marginal figure in the various narratives about Port William, suddenly emerges within the shape of the membership upon the death of Mat Feltner. At the end of the story "That Distant Land," when the news of Mat's death has reached the men in the field, "nobody yet knew what to say. We did not know what we were going to do. We were, I finally realized,

25. "Conserving Communities," in ATC, 11–12.
26. "People, Land, Community," in ACP, 185.

waiting on Jarrat. It was Elton's farm, but Jarrat was now the oldest man, and we were waiting on him" (TDL, 318).

But today there are fewer and fewer moments of clear cultural demarcation such as happens on that dirt road with Jarrat Coulter. We experience the loss of a celebrity much more sharply than the loss of a neighbor. And when the destruction of community results in the loss of local character and the collapse of local culture, the alternative offered everyone is a kind of homogenous "anticulture." Individuals are forced into an anonymous loop of cell phones, subdivisions, strip malls, satellite TV shows—everything except for shared, relational, human living. The illusion is that ominous security we feel in being able to enter any mall or fast-food chain anywhere in America, or around the world for that matter, without any sense of displacement and dislocation. My (Matt's) visit to a mall in Belo Horizonte, Brazil, in 2006 was scary in the familiarity and homogeneity of shops, smells, and sights that I've encountered in American malls. What small-town dweller in the 1980s didn't feel a spike of "civic pride" in the arrival of a McDonald's or a cable TV service? Likewise, at the turn of the millennium the coming of the Super Wal-Mart or, for the more urbane, a Starbuck's kiosk in a local store seems a harbinger of hope and global relevance. But tragically—and each of us could list a dozen towns that witnessed that dynamic, and a dozen more that have been passed over and emptied out by the gravitational pull of commerce—the artificiality of this promise produces superficial character and consumeristic culture. Our comfort in becoming relevant ends up producing the ultimate dislocation. The genuine human interaction that is central to open-air street markets is replaced with the trite chitchat of the mall clerk.

Berry often reveals this tension in the economic activity of a community—nothing epitomizes us as Americans more than our economic hyperactivity. We are a buying and selling, producing and consuming juggernaut, leveling every activity by imposing our "right to choose." This attitude of ownership and earning is in direct conflict with an attitude of gift and gratitude, and hence our economic practices reveal our attitude toward creation. This is bigger than just a desire to "shop till you drop"; it is manifested in undisciplined, shallow paths upon which we find ourselves unformed or deformed.

But this is not beyond reversal. In the midst of such peril, we want to keep pointing to the healing possibilities that Berry suggests. A tremendously vital local culture can still be created and sustained, but it will take much more work than surrendering to the abstract, homogenous trope of culture that now dominates. At the local level, we must reassert that character matters far more than choice and thus reorient the deep motives by which we live. When Berry suggests, at the end of "Conserving Communities," a set of rules for "how a sustainable local community (which is to say a sustainable local economy) might function," he frames them in terms of creating coherence, of seeing the layers working together ("If the members of a local community want their community to cohere, to flourish, and to last, these are some things they would do").[27] Rule 2 notes the range of layers to be considered: "Always include local nature—the land, the water, the air, the native creatures—within the membership of the community." Likewise, the notion of coherence reaches into the realm of stewardship in Rule 11: "Make the community able to invest in itself by maintaining its properties, keeping itself clean (without dirtying some other place), caring for its old people, teaching its children."[28] Like so many of Berry's statements, this is a simple list to read but complex and arduous to undertake. His instruction to us is always a tacit challenge to our habituations.

Berry admits this difficulty freely in the essay "The Purpose of a Coherent Community." Here he pinpoints what health would look like and shows the impossibility of a piecemeal approach to the various layers and strands of local culture: "For the parts can be reconciled to one another only within the pattern of the whole thing to which they belong. . . . Only the purpose of a coherent community, fully alive both in the world and in the minds of its members, can carry us beyond fragmentation, contradiction and negativity,

27. ATC, 18–19.
28. Ibid., 19–20.

teaching us to preserve, not in opposition but in affirmation and affection, all things needful to make us glad to live."[29] Berry deepens the discussion on the priority of local community when he suggests the necessity not only of embodiment but also of a reimagining of such structures. There is an intentionality in this that will require us to think deliberately about what we are attempting, rather than merely reappropriating some communal past. The key again is an embrace of mutuality and gratitude, since "the members of a community cohere on the basis of their recognized need for one another, a need that is in many ways practical but never utilitarian."[30] Thus coherence is natural, not programmed or controlled from any central enterprise. But it must be cultivated, constantly and consistently nurtured, by those whose characters are at stake. The coherent local community is rooted in a natural order that gets elevated into the human order by means of recognition and response to healthy desires. Every time a neighbor, or a town board, or a local business, or a corner church acts in such a way as to foster the particular community members, there is a strengthening of the internal magnetism that holds the community together.

But we cannot ignore the brutal, polarizing magnetism of so much economic activity away from the local toward the industrialized, globalized abstraction that we serve but never come to know. If economics is ultimately not about choice but about character, then Berry wants to assert the necessity of choices that are recklessly countermodern, boldly constrained, and vulnerable, strongly anchored in a particular place among specific people: "If it is to cohere, a community cannot agree to the loss of any of its members, or the disemployment of any of its members, as an acceptable cost of an economic program. If it is to cohere, a community must remember its history and its obligations; it is therefore irreconcilably opposed to 'mobility' as a social norm. Persons, places, and things have a practical value, but they are not reducible to such value; they are not interchangeable. That is why we outlawed slavery. That is why a house

29. WI, 77–78.
30. Ibid., 79.

for sale is not a home."[31] To believe that *obligation* is not a pejorative word, that it is in fact a blessed word and a life-giving notion, will require a great shift for us all, and not just of semantics.

To shun our obligations creates precisely the irresponsible dependence that never leads to health. In the world of Port William, this tension is played out when it comes to renters and hired hands, those who don't own the land and thus are in a tenuous relationship to their place. Whereas obligation in such a context might simply mean a contractual arrangement of vocational duties and timely pay, the notion is nuanced by Berry to include the fragile but crucial possibility of respect and membership, even for the marginalized. For some families, such as the Banions, a black family that has worked for decades for the Feltners, the commitment to place and to the community is both given and reciprocated—the Banions do their work and tend their place with integrity, and the Feltners give them respect and friendship, opening a way into the healing community. But the next tenants in the old Banion house, Lightning Berlew and his wife, represent a shirking of obligations, a refusal to connect at all with place and people, a resistance to any feeling of obligation. Lightning's obsession with keeping his car running, precisely so that the family can escape the farm on Saturday nights (and leave town without warning, eventually, shearing away all obligation) is sharply contrasted with the Banions' at-homeness. Here we see the whole range of the fragile possibilities of usufruct—not all renters are bad, but there is a danger built in when no connection is made to land, people, or community.

A more intimate, and more painful, resistance to obligation appears in the novel *Hannah Coulter*, as Hannah laments the utter disconnection her grandkids feel toward not only the farm but toward her, its steward. Seeing them shying from the barn and livestock and instead sitting indoors playing with their Game Boys, Hannah broods: "Whatever in their lives will they think of the old woman. . . . My love for Mattie's children . . . is a failed love, and hard to bear."[32]

31. WI, 79.
32. HC, 125.

In Hannah's reflections, we see that the obligations of community are not simply issues of bloodlines and ancestral lands; there is no guarantee that proximity will lead to the recognition of these obligations. Likewise, these obligations can be carried in one's bosom to a new place, as long as it is an actual place and not just a stopover. Many of us have been displaced multiple times in our lives, by education, by jobs, by marriage, by seemingly random courses of events. The question for most of us is not "Should we return to the house of our childhood?" By now there might be a score of such houses, or none. But we can ask, "How do we enact the obligations of community and home in the place where we find ourselves?" As Berry reminds us, we must start where we are, and we're all somewhere.

We—Matt and Michael—each live about a nine-hour drive from where we grew up and where our families more or less still dwell. For Matt that is southeastern Ohio, in the region just north of the Ohio River. For Michael that is Upstate New York, in the hills just south of the Finger Lakes. Both of our homelands are small-town and rural, both are agricultural districts, both have great natural beauty, yet we both live in western Michigan and intend to stay where we are. Have we violated Berry's tenets for community? It seems instead that Berry suggests we must create "healing communities" wherever we find ourselves, that we must make mature decisions at some point to lay down roots, stretch out branches, and seek to find the "coherence" available to us within the boundaries (often nearly invisible) that we must locate and respect. The "membership of Port William" that constitutes Berry's fundamental model of community is not, in fact, wholly genetic. Some of the most important figures in it—Jayber Crow, Elton and Mary Penn, Hannah Coulter—have come from the outside, have been orphans of sorts, adopted in. Also, many of the townspeople's direct descendants depart and never return except as visitors. So neither lifelong proximity nor genetics but a sort of mutual at-homeness is at the root of community. To claim this is to understand the soil we stand on, ourselves embodied and finite, and the nature of the connections we share, as well as the limits. It is an awareness of the gift.

One final ingredient in the healing community is love. Such a community is ultimately rooted in a love that gives and calls, that is born of mortality and limitation, that comes with expectations and obligations. In "Health Is Membership" Berry says, "Earthly love seeks plenitude. It longs for the full membership to be present and to be joined. The difference between divine love and earthly love is that earthly love does not have the power, knowledge and will to achieve what it longs for . . . to be comprehensive and effective enough."[33] So living within the sharp limits of our fallenness and our creatureliness, we are mitigated by community.

We need to remember that these are two different sorts of limits, requiring differing responses. A conflation is possible between these two sorts of limits, the latter built into creation, the former resulting from sin, and perhaps Berry tends to conflate them. In response to creaturely limits, we are called to humility and gratitude, to finding our place within the given order. In response to sin's limits, or perhaps more appropriately sin's limitations upon us, we are to work toward freedom from sin's captivity and toward the further redemptive work of setting free the captives. Trying to figure out which limits are to be embraced and which are to be fought, protested, lamented—this is cloudy and confounding work, easily discouraging.[34] But we can't give up the measuring and weighing and working, for we must find and foster healing boundaries if we are to thrive. The only way to find healing communities, and thence to foster them, is to wrestle with these distinctions together.

This chapter has been a discussion about community primarily, which is the end in mind for a context of healing. But Berry's genius is in showing the means, the steps along the way that we must take without losing the vision for the end. We now have a glimpse why the wilderness sustains us, why we are embodied, why we love and bond together. But we also see that community must be bounded. If

---

33. ACP, 153.

34. Hannah Coulter also reflects on this poignantly: "You can't give yourself to love for somebody without giving yourself over to suffering. . . . You wake in the night to the thought of the hurt and the helpless, the scorned and cheated, . . . the spit upon, the shit upon," (HC, 171).

we describe community as the acceptance and giving of love within permeable boundaries, if we assert along with Berry that "no loved one is standardized,"[35] then maybe we can find our place within the "wild spaces of love."[36] In the next chapter we will ponder what this means for the status of the individual in a globalized world—what sorts of tensions and difficulties are involved in sustaining the healing community. For Berry, health is to be measured by the citizens themselves, and hence civic activity involves those who are bounded together into a community and whose relationships can be seen to promote either health or disease: "There is no such thing as a global village. No matter how much we may love the world as a whole, one can live fully in it only by living responsibly in some small part of it. We thus come to the paradox that one can become whole only by the responsible acceptance of one's partiality."[37]

In the end, we must address the twin questions "What's too small?" and "What's too large?" By focusing on local community, Berry offers a place of authentic human interaction that neither the uncultivated desire of individualism nor the abstract ideal of globalism can promise. The problems of the autonomous self have been identified by many, yet the persistence of this fundamental way of constructing meaning puts it firmly in Berry's crosshairs as well. The opposite error of loss of distinction within the totalizing forces of globalization is a newer phenomenon that seems to us particularly dangerous, since it usurps the very notion of the local. Beyond a certain scale of human interaction, social structures have a tendency to become fictionalized as "*the* Market" or "*the* State"; hence, the ability to judge humanly and appropriately is clouded. Though economies and political entities can and should exist beyond the local community, there will always be a tendency toward usurpation and subjugation of the local, to the destruction of real people in real places.

---

35. "Health Is Membership," in ACP, 154.
36. James Olthuis, *The Beautiful Risk* (Grand Rapids: Zondervan, 2001), 12.
37. ACP, 117–18.

# 7

## Healing Individualism,
## Healing Globalism?

If Berry's notion of a local and finite community helps to provide the roots for our constructive venture, it is nonetheless the case that a healing community, like anything else well ordered by humans, is in need of constant nurturing. It's no longer "good soil" that needs cultural tending; now the "soil" is rank with weeds and poisons of our own making. We discern two current threats to healing communities. The first is a tendency toward a consumer-driven autonomous individualism—the eighteenth-century vision of individuals guided by natural laws distorted into a self-seeking paradigm, guided only by the plentitude of individual desire. The second tendency is toward a radical globalization, a reaching beyond any prior limitations, a move that is ironically a consequence of the elevation of the individual as consumer. The ever-increasing supply-and-demand cycle, if it is to be sustained at low prices and high efficiencies, must continually push through and erase any local boundaries, however healthy their previous manifestations. The end emerging from this distortion is a homogenous culture that is no longer defined by any local geography, local stories, or local virtues.

The two directions are both abstractions, both part of the same problem, which is the avoidance of other persons-in-community in the calculus of one's well-being. The two poles begin to look more like a loop of disease, a parasitic cycle whereby self-interest demands access to the world while shunning any accountability to that world. So how do these two powerful polar directions work to undermine true community, and how can communities keep from being flattened?[1]

Recall chapter 2's survey of all the various ideological camps that seem drawn to Wendell Berry's ideas. Jeffrey Stout has argued that Berry stands at a nexus of movements in social criticism. To return to our own metaphor, Berry represents the weaving together of a patchwork vision offering the possibility that both individuals connecting locally and communities connecting globally can be redemptive. In fact, individuals, households, communities, and the vast web of "communities of communities" that make up human society must work in a sort of symbiosis with one another; but without the stabilizing locus of the healing community, this symbiosis can easily warp into parasitism. Berry's path into these concerns is sometimes through direct historical and sociological commentary but more often and more compellingly by renarrating our understanding of the relationship of self and world. The healing community is thus the place of possibility, where every individual everywhere in the world might have a chance to be wholly with him- or herself and wholly with the other.

For both classic conservatives and postmodernists, Berry points toward root narratives that offer something more than the homogenous account of human community that modernity provides. Neither movement wants to see human beings as disembodied rational agents, purely transactional beings. But the two movements diverge from each other rather quickly. For the classic conservative, the problem with community comes when it is seen as sublimating individual freedom, whereas for the postmodernist the problem stems from an anxiety with any imposed boundaries on community, which

1. As an example of globalization's ability to undermine community, see Thomas Friedman's book *The World Is Flat: A Brief History of the Twenty-first Century* (New York: Farrar, Straus, and Giroux, 2006).

are seen as coercive and violent. Yet this postmodern tendency is not synonymous with the urge toward globalization—though globalization breaks down boundaries, the motive of consumerism is more a product of hyper-modernity, individualism run amok. The postmodern fluidity of boundary is rather a move of reaction to the violence of imposed identifiers—it is suspicious of ready-made identity. Such a resistance has created within postmodern discourse an affinity with mystery that was utterly absent from modernity, though it is still only thinly connected to the creational mystery toward which Berry doggedly points. Whereas Berry's mystery is embodied and particularized all around us, in human relations and the natural order, the postmodern sense of mystery remains remote and unnamable.

Likewise, the libertarian strand of conservatism shies from mystery, but voices such as Russell Kirk's seem open to the mystery of tradition, of ethereal but irrevocable rootedness. This comes close, in its sweep, to Berry's vision of the healing community, but not quite. Berry's creational mystery keeps a steadfast emphasis on particularity. He focuses on neither the public nor the individual exclusively, but he is not dismissive of the role and importance of either. He sees their place, but only in the flourishing of healthy local communities can the individual be properly connected to the world, and vice versa. Only in communities are *people* cultivated into *citizens*. There are no shortcuts in either direction, at least none that bring life and health. Starting with identity understood primarily as individual freedom is just as debilitating as starting with global connectedness. In both cases there is a use for the other, but in both it is difficult to recognize the *gift* of the other.

## Fragile Individualism

Berry's agrarianism is not that of rugged individualism: "the tragic version of rugged individualism is in the presumptive 'right' of individuals to be able to do as they please, as if there were no God, no legitimate government, no community, no neighbors, and no posterity."[2] Nor is his the vision of the Jeffersonian gentleman-farmer per se—it is not the individual as emancipated being that can sustain a vital connection to place. Berry sees a radical fork in the road with regard to what might evolve: either the posthuman world mediated only through technology and devoid of any reality of place (dependent on superimposable virtual constructs) or a world of members and neighbors connected with creation and each other. No bridges can span this divide.

An appropriate individuality, then, has its desires molded by obligations to the other, within the boundaries of community. Berry cites instances of civil disobedience from Thoreau onward as positive possibilities: "This is individualism of a kind rugged enough, and it has been authenticated typically by its identification with a communal good."[3] This includes a training of desires and shaping of character, rather than an autonomous pursuit of self-fulfillment. Such individuality makes possible the strong relationships found within the "membership" of Port William. An appropriate self-interest keeps perspective and proportion regarding one's individual work and labor. But here, as anywhere, we see this most clearly when the boundaries are breached. For Jack Beechum, a longing to find utter independence through sheer force of sweat on his farm leads not only to a warping of relationship with the land (especially when he extends its boundaries) but also, and more important, a breaking of relationship with his wife and daughter and with the community around him. Only in his old age, when he submits (at times quite grudgingly) to the kindness and hospitality of friends, do we see him completely within the orb of the "membership."

This struggle to learn to receive the gift of "membership," to learn that a fully fledged sense of self does not mean passive reception nor solitary labors—this is the difficulty that many of the young people of Port William (and everywhere else) must face. Some learn more quickly than others. In the short story "A Jonquil for Mary Penn" we meet a young couple who reappear again and again in Berry's

2. "Rugged Individualism," in WI, 9.
3. Ibid.

fiction, especially Elton Penn, whose story extends from his early days as a neighbor boy of Tol Proudfoot through his manhood as the hardest-working member of the community, the heir figuratively and also literally of Old Jack's legacy. In "A Jonquil for Mary Penn" the Penns are recently married, living on a hardscrabble farm, without parental support (Elton is an orphan, Mary has been disowned by her socially conscious family for marrying beneath her station). During a morning of illness Mary ruminates on the early travails of marriage. She is fascinated and a little scared by Elton's fierce independence: "When a neighbor had offered him crop ground, room, and wages, he had taken charge of himself and, though he was still a boy, he had become a man. He wanted, he said, to have to say thank you to nobody. Or to nobody but her."[4] Though the Penns live on a ridge with a set of nurturing and generous farm families, though Elton receives much of his education in farming from the likes of Walter Cotman and Tom Hardy, and though Mary is taken under the wings of the genial wives, Elton's yearning for independence creates ongoing tension.

When he's told that Josie Braymer is the best tobacco cutter of the whole bunch, Elton misses the gentle irony of the situation and interprets it as a challenge. Thus, he vows that he'll be first to the end of the tobacco row, and "when he got there [the end of the row] Josie Braymer was not, and neither was any of the men. It was not that he did not want to be bested by a woman; he did not want to be bested by anybody. One thing Mary would never have to do was wonder which way he was. She knew he would rather die than be beaten."[5] His perfectionism breeds brooding anger: "When he failed, he was like the sun in a cloud, alone and burning, furious in his doubt, furious at her because she trusted in him though he doubted."[6] Though their marital love is fresh and powerful—"when had there ever been such a yearning of halves toward each other, such a longing, even

4. "A Jonquil for Mary Penn," in *Fidelity*, 66.
5. Ibid., 77.
6. Ibid., 78–79.

in quarrels, to be whole?"[7]—the end of the narrative finds Mary lamenting that the power of their passion is not enough, that "now that wholeness was not imaginable; she felt herself a part without counterpart, a mere fragment of something unknown, dark and broken off."[8] We see how isolating individualism can be destructive: the potential seasoning of the broader community is present, but Elton is not yet able to fully receive the gift.

But then Berry, in one of his finest narrative twists, opens the door upon the final scene: the ill and listless Mary, having allowed the fires to go out in her misery, awakens to a warm house and the presence of her neighbor Josie Tom, maternal and hospitable as she stitches her embroidery:

> And so Mary knew all the story of her day. Elton, going by Josie Tom's in the half-light, had stopped and called.
> She could hear his voice, raised to carry through the wind: "Mrs. Hardy, Mary's sick, and I have to go over to Walter's to plow."
> So he had known. He had thought of her. He had told Josie Tom.[9]

The story's charming finale reveals much more about the nature of "membership" than about the satisfactions of young lovers. That Elton puts aside his ambitions, lowers his guard to ask a neighbor to sit in his place, as it were, is an amazing gesture. That Mary recognizes it for exactly the sacrifice and extension out of self that it is provides a fitting closure to the story. The Penns have community, need community, can find their wholeness together only through the community. Though some of their deepest individual longings are fulfilled within marriage and household (in spite of Elton's struggles with pride and self-sufficiency), they must move beyond household to really be at home.

Berry asserts that " 'Every man for himself' is a doctrine for a feeding frenzy or for a panic in a burning nightclub, appropriate for

7. Ibid., 79.
8. Ibid.
9. Ibid, 81.

sharks or hogs or perhaps a cascade of lemmings. A society wishing to endure must speak the language of care-taking, faith-keeping, kindness, neighborliness, and peace. That language is another precious resource that cannot be 'privatized.' "[10] He leaves no room for an isolated, and isolating, individualism, even if the language of social Darwinism is all we hear or have ever heard. In a phrasing reminiscent of Orwell's cautions, Berry suggests that if we cannot even speak healthily, we'll no longer be able to imagine, and certainly will never figure out, how to embody the health we need.

## Tugging at the Boundaries

Individualism has one set of perils, but just as dangerous is the dissolving of the individual into a shapeless, generalized, corporately constructed global entity. Berry takes to task the cultural tendency of erasing any boundaries that might preserve a place for local community, making it always subordinate to the global. Strangely—or maybe these paradoxes are not so strange anymore—the tendency toward dehumanizing and depersonifying that follows in the wake of expansive corporatization has actually come in the guise of individualist language. Berry points out the duplicity that is afoot "when great corporations are granted the status of 'persons,' who then can also become rugged individuals, insisting on their right to do whatever they please with their property."[11]

In the global context Berry identifies two new threats to healthy community, both of which have to do with inappropriate construction of communal boundaries. The consequences for American communities are evident both economically and politically; either borders exist only to be breached by trade, or they are created to insulate and isolate in order to "make life safe" through political-economic-military means. Such borders end up either too soft or too hard, or at once somehow both. The one thing that becomes most elusive,

10. WI, 11.
11. Ibid., 9–10.

then, is a boundary that fosters life in the way Berry has suggested it must be fostered.

Borders and boundaries are much on Berry's mind in his analysis of the U.S. National Security Policy of 2002, which was crafted in response to the 9/11 attacks. Berry identifies two Americas—or maybe it is better to say that he identifies two direction-giving forces at work in American society. For the first force Berry uses a phrase that dates from at least Calvin Coolidge: there is an America whose "business is business." The concern of this America in an age of globalization is the protection of open channels of trade. Porous national borders (economically, if not physically) make global trade more efficient, permitting quicker response to demand. By the time you have gotten home from Wal-Mart with your new shirt, a replacement is likely already on its way to the store. The "just-in-time" market demands a free flow of lower-cost goods into the American market so that stock is quickly replenished. Yet such a border has nothing to do with the boundaries that sustain healing. This is not a permeability that is healthy for discourse and hospitality. The holes are not people-sized, only product-sized.

In contrast to the market's demand for a porous border, the other threatening force leads to a desire for a perimeter that cannot be penetrated. Especially after 9/11, the America whose business is military strength showcases its technological prowess, its new political powers, and its willingness to go great distances to keep violence from our shores. In order to make us safe, our borders, in a sense, can even be extended into other nations through preemptive acts of violence. Rather than serving to protect the finitude within which which relationships can be forged and deepened, these boundaries leap past any healthy understanding of limit. The result is a redefinition of patriotism, or a reaffirmation of a definition that has endured since World War I, where the abstract principle of "freedom" or "making the world safe for democracy" replaces any particular object of defense. As Berry explains in "A Citizen's Response to 'The National Security Strategy of the United States of America,'" we must always particularize our loyalties: "An inescapable requirement of true patriotism, love for one's land, is a vigilant distrust of any determinative power, elected or unelected, that may preside over it."[12]

Berry's reading points out a basic tension in America's self-understanding: the cooperation of a global economy and a military with a global reach in the "flat world" that Thomas Friedman has articulated. Although Friedman and Berry would utterly disagree on first principles—for the former this flattening is the harbinger of a golden age, for the latter it is a heinous force of destruction—both see that the eventual effect of current practices will be a steamrolling of any and all local boundaries. Here we see a kind of global market contract as an extension of the social contract of classical liberalism. Thus the market contract is an extension of the classical liberal view of the self. In the midst of such conflations, where the nation-state ends and the market-state begins, the question of which props up which remains foggy. What is not difficult to ascertain is that in both states concerns of local community will be utterly subordinated to the global.

Berry's call for a return to the local is sensitive to particularity. When consumerism erases boundaries and when, in the name of efficiency, the particular topography of a given place is bulldozed flat by economic progress and military might, the idea of the local must be defended. Berry insists on situating our interactions, our exchanges, in a place of real implications for real people. By rooting the discussion in the local, we begin to see the multitude of experiences and connections that humans in community share, that cannot be marketed or abstracted. When you shop at Wal-Mart or Target or any of the "big-box stores," the only possible connection you gain is a momentary encounter with a clerk (though automated check-outs, if you can learn to navigate them, are rendering even this final human frontier obsolete). Every other possible connection is rendered abstract almost immediately, leaving just money and

---

12. CZP, 5. We thank Chris Allers once again here for noting that Berry's articulation is a gloss of none other than the aforementioned George Orwell, who states in *Notes on Nationalism*: "By 'patriotism' I mean devotion to a particular place and a particular way of life, which one believes to be the best in the world but has no wish to force on other people."

products flying across a vast commercial hyperspace. A move to local businesses makes both people and product more concrete, even if more expensive, more unwieldy, less convenient. Berry's tenet that one should attempt to keep money and the loop of products and commerce as close to home as can be creatively achieved, is more than just a economic renewal strategy. He knows what we begin to suspect, that the investment in one another will not remain merely economic exchange but will be move toward healthy dependence, appropriate obligation—in short, community. Somewhat more provocative, though very urgent at the moment of our writing as gasoline soars above $4 a gallon, is the troubling interweaving of economic and military tensions between our own nation and the major oil-producing countries. Not all dependence is healthy!

Berry's conception of the local is persuasive because it allows exactly what the totalizing tendency of the global market disallows: a recognition of particularity. And with this recognition comes the possibility of hearing the voices of the other, in time and in place and in person. While Berry rarely speaks in explicit terms of justice, he does point to a way of living in the world that can't be based merely on tolerance. This is why he attempts, in "The Purpose of a Coherent Community," to articulate the conditions for a just community in terms of coherence: "If it is to cohere, a community must remember its history and its obligation; it is therefore irreconcilably opposed to 'mobility' as a social norm. Persons, places, and things have a practical value, but are not reducible to such value; they are not interchangeable."[13] In this final sentence, Berry points again to the mystery of creational value, to a bounded vision of just human interaction that cannot be encapsulated by either the political or the economic.

But the enemy of such boundedness is elusive because it has become a spirit of the age, or, in Berry's terms, "a political faith for which there is no justification." Berry defines this notion of a "sentimental capitalism" in his essay "The Idea of a Local Economy": "[It] holds in effect that everything small, local, private, personal, natural, good,

13. WI, 79.

and beautiful must be sacrificed in the interest of the 'free market' and the great corporations, which will bring unprecedented security and happiness to 'the many'—in, of course, the future."[14] This is embodied today in a "global economy" that is "the property of a few supranational corporations." In such a system, efficiency "always means reducing labor costs by replacing workers with cheaper workers or with machines."[15] The implicit depersonalization of this spiritual system becomes explicit as people themselves are eliminated or subjugated because they are no longer practical. The erasure of the local and the community results in a paradox: the more global we become, the more isolated and individualistic we become. The typical worker within the global economy can't see any of the connections that might make his work meaningful; all that is left is his own desires and devices. This is perhaps a dark and negative version of mystery, this anonymous and untraceable mode of global exchange.

The only way back from this is a recognition of the limits that define your work and the relationship of your work to other work—this sense of connectedness is the entry point to membership and care. The term *membership* that Berry keeps returning to carries in it the healing tension of gift and obligation. In fact, in "Health is Membership," Berry sees that the vulnerability in membership is its strength. The promised security of global political and economic forces is provided only at the cost of making both us and our enemies inhuman. "In the world of love, things separated by efficiency and specialization strive to come back together. And yet love must confront death, and accept it, and learn from it. Only in confronting death can earthly love learn its true extent, its immortality."[16] We are back to the notion of limits as healing forces, boundaries as the necessary antecedents to health. If we willingly surrender our self-protection and vast access to things and turn instead toward those around us in gratitude and humility, we have made the move toward health, membership, and belonging.

14. ACP, 251.
15. Ibid., 254.
16. ACP, 155.

Berry's portrayal of the path to membership in his fiction emphasizes humility, the humility of the apprentice who sees what the master can offer and who is willing to take the time, maybe a lifetime, to glean it. There is nothing formal about such a process, but it is part of the warp and woof of local community. In the story "It Wasn't Me," we encounter Elton Penn again, ten years into his marriage and at the end of a tutelage to Jack Beechum, his landlord and patron, who has just died. Jack wants Elton and Mary to have his land and has bequeathed them enough money to make a beginning at paying for it—they had worked it to his martinet's satisfaction for a few years already and had gained his trust. But complications ensue when Jack's citified daughter and her banker husband, Clara and Glad Pettit, arrive from Louisville seeking a maximum price for the property. Elton bids beyond his means at the behest of the lawyer Wheeler Catlett, champion and guardian of the "Port William membership." All this drama ends in Elton's purchase of the land but also his irritation that he's had to become obliged to Wheeler in the purchasing. Things are tense when Elton meets Wheeler in the law office later, but there is also an unveiling, a sort of ceremony of induction. Part of their exchange gives a glimpse of this, as Elton states:

> "I want to make it on my own. I don't want a soul to thank."
>
> Wheeler thinks, "Too late," but he does not say it. He grins. That he knows the futility of that particular program does not prevent him from liking it. "Well," he says, "putting aside whatever Mary Penn might have to say about that, and putting aside what it means in the first place just to be a living human, I don't think your old friend has left you in shape to live thankless."
>
> He sees that Elton sees, or is beginning to. This man who longs to be independent cannot bear to be ungrateful. Wheeler knows that. But the suffering of obligation is still on Elton, and he says, "What do you mean?"
>
> "I mean you're a man indebted to a dead man. So am I. So was he. That's the story of it. Back of you is Jack Beechum. Back of him was

138

Ben Feltner. Back of him was, I think, his own daddy. And back of him somebody else, and on back that way, who knows how far? . . ."

"Well, how did I get in it?" Elton says almost in a sigh, as if longing to be out of it.

"The way you got in it, I guess, was by being chosen. The way you stay in it is by choice. . . . And then we'd have to say that, through him the farm chose you."

Elton looks straight at him. "The *farm* did."

Wheeler smiles. "The land expects something from us. The line of succession, the true line, is the membership of people who know it does. Uncle Jack knew it, and he knew you would learn it."[17]

Somewhere in this mystery, of earning and yet receiving a gift, of choosing yet also being chosen, of a yearning for independence and alongside a burgeoning knowledge of the debt to community, people living and dead—somewhere in there is the key to "membership," as Berry casts it, both in the winsome world of Port William and in our own worlds.[18]

Some fail to ever gain it, others come to it late. There's a proving ground of sorts, but membership has mainly to do with care of the land and willingness to be responsible for each other. Jack Beechum must show Ben Feltner that he belongs, Elton Penn must show Jack, Andy Catlett must show Elton eventually. This debt cannot ever be paid in economic terms but is rather paid by entering into the obligations—past, present, and future—of this set of relationships. The concern of the members is often with those less "at home," still trying to find their place. Instead of economic exchange, we find the mysterious work of grace. This is the sort of bounded and healing community that we must all desire, no matter what context or forces constrain us. Ultimately, it's the offer of a good life of mutuality, both obligated and free, at odds with "the Good Life" of upward mobility, which isolates and enslaves.

17. "It Wasn't Me," in TDL, 283–84.

18. As Wheeler says to Elton a bit earlier in the exchange from "It Wasn't Me," "The place . . . is not its price. Its price stands for it for just a minute or two while it's bought and sold, and may hang over it a while after that and have an influence on it, but the place has been here since the evening and the morning were the third day" (TDL, 282).

Humility is not just a personal virtue here, a simple emptying of oneself. There is a humility of place as well, a satisfaction with where one is instead of the quest always for something bigger, better, purer: "In a viable neighborhood, neighbors ask themselves what they can do or provide for one another, and they find answers that they and their place can afford."[19] Neighborhood here is akin to what we've been calling local community, but we must note Berry is careful with this term: "Community must mean a people locally placed and a people, moreover, not too numerous to have a common knowledge of themselves and their place."[20] Furthermore, community exists "by a conscientious granting of trust . . . it knows face-to-face, and it trusts as it knows."[21] This interdependence once again points to vulnerability, to the "giving away" of self and the simultaneous reception of the gift of the other. This sort of exchange, so different from the faceless economic exchange of the global market and the abstract citizenhood of modern nation-states, makes for health and wholeness.

The healthy boundaries of local community appropriately resist the individualism and the globalism that would render the very community meaningless. Yet they are permeable to the healthy human exchange represented by hospitality, invitation, care, and gratitude. Such boundedness makes connection possible but also constantly challenges the spirit within modern humanity for limitlessness. Our longing for security must be satisfied in the constructing of healthy communities, not in preparations for threat and exclusion. The fact that healthy boundaries have to be permeable creates a vulnerable dynamic; wherever appropriate connections are possible, so are breakages and abstractions away from community, and hence away from health. In such a context, the chief virtue may well be hospitality, but this goes far beyond a simple "howdy, folks" greeting at the door. A healing hospitality will need to be stronger, more flexible, more resilient. In the next chapter we'll survey a cross-section of just such a hospitality, lived out by the characters in Berry's fictional world of Port William.

19. "The Idea of a Local Economy," in ACP, 260.
20. "Sex, Economy, Freedom, and Community," in ACP, 178.
21. Ibid., 174.

# 8

· · · · · · · · · · · ·

# An Invitation to Hospitality

## A Place at the Table

Localness is thus the crucial limit, but the notion would be incomplete, and likely misleading, without an understanding of the boundaries as permeable. Permeability here means an authentic, embodied meeting of human beings, rather than just a transference of goods, services, and information. If the apertures are people-sized, then there is opportunity for hospitality to be both extended and embraced. For healthy community to exist, such hospitality must be possible. People must be able to come as they are, without being forced into any role or niche except that which naturally evolves as the whole community shifts to make room. Much depends upon the initial gestures of hospitality at the boundaries where exclusion, rejection, and even exile are the easier responses. In Berry's world, initial hospitality often involves a temporary or provisional entry into the membership of place and relationships by some "other." In order to take such a risk, the community must already have a measure of health, and hospitality is the pulse of such health, proof of willingness to be vulnerable. As we've argued, the extension of politics and economics at the expense of the local can be predicated only upon an unhealthy sense of community that is fundamentally inhospitable in its dependence on competition and violence toward the unknown "other." The "other" is outside the boundaries of care and at best unrecognized, at worst abused and destroyed. This is often an apathetic exclusion, couched in terms of protecting our own. The "other" at the boundary, whether it be the marginalized developing-world factory worker, the immigrant (legal or illegal) working at the construction site or meat-packing plant or lettuce field, or the harried middle manager in the constantly shifting, Darwinian corporation, moves in a world outside the boundary of care.

As an aside that deserves much further unpacking, one of the most provocative responses to this exclusionary and violent territorialism in politics and economics has been the postmodern, postindustrial concern for the other arising in the work of late-twentieth-century thinkers such as Emmanuel Levinas and Jacques Derrida.[1] Familiar with the horrifying margins that the twentieth century harbored, such ideologists have responded with anxiety toward all boundaries, which they see as inherently violent and as statements of biased self-protection. Such claims seem radical but are hard to dismiss when the dark proofs are all around us in the world news and in our own hometowns. Though we stand with Berry in affirming the necessity of hospitality, as embodied in places like Port William, we are still forced to ask how it can be practiced in Darfur, Kosovo, Myanmar, Beirut, or the inner cities of America. The witness of Levinas and Derrida shatters the complacency of those of us who are far from the violence, but in a strange way they also affirm Berry's vision, because he too questions how we can still strive to be cultured, ordered, virtuous, and hospitable in such a fractured world. In fact, where Levinas and Derrida see the only meaningful response to violence and exclusion in our world as a sacrificial offering of the self and its

1. Jamie Smith is a very helpful reader of these two thinkers, particularly his essay "The Call as Gift: The Subject's Donation in Marion and Levinas" in the volume he edited with Henry Venema, *The Hermeneutics of Charity* (Grand Rapids: Brazos, 2004), and his book *Derrida: Live Theory* (London: Continuum, 2005), where he plumbs the depths of Derrida's evolving thoughts on the self/other tension.

set of desires, we follow Berry in asserting the hope of community, realized where neither self nor other is lost.[2]

How does Berry the fiction writer, the "world maker" in J. R. R. Tolkien's parlance, reveal the centrality of hospitality in the fabric of his created universe? He begins with a natural connection between member selves—there is a community (the origin of which we never quite know) with households, families, characters in place and interacting. It is a stable but dynamic world, the boundaries sustaining the living community while always offering the permeability that both risks and reveals such life. No particular character dominates, no signature hero, Berry's point seemingly being the necessity of recognizing the space for mutuality, the bounded space wherein members can share themselves. In a sense, the community itself *is* the protagonist of Berry's fiction.

This seems to be a good moment for establishing a fuller context for Berry's fictional world, which we've mentioned periodically throughout this book. The span of Berry's history of Port William reaches from stories set in the late nineteenth century, with reminiscences stretching back to the Civil War, all the way to the year 2000, with the novel *Hannah Coulter*. Nearly all the short stories have been collected in a single volume, *That Distant Land*, where they are placed in chronological order, with notation in the table of contents as to where the handful of novels and novellas fit as well. But Berry's method over his nearly fifty years of crafting Port William has been the furthest thing from such an ordered and streamlined epic. Instead, he has worked discursively, looping back and forth through time and space and characters, sometimes all within the same work. Many of the works center on the time of Berry's own boyhood and adolescence, around the Depression and World War II and the coming of full mechanization to the farm, a time of both affirmation and testing of the power of the local community to hold

2. Jim Olthuis has also offered an acute reading of Levinas and Derrida in "Ethical Asymmetry or the Symmetry of Mutuality?" from a volume he edited, *Knowing Other-Wise* (New York: Fordham University Press, 1997): "The dance of mutuality is always drenched in vulnerability and risk because it is a non-coerced meeting of two free subjects in the wild spaces of love" (147).

itself together as the world falls asunder. Two of the early novels, *Nathan Coulter* and *A Place on Earth*, hark back to this time, as does the more recent *Andy Catlett: Early Travels*. In between sit the wide-ranging narratives of *The Memory of Old Jack*, set in the 1950s but ranging over the sixty years of success and failure of Jack Beechum, the archetypal farmer, and *Jayber Crow*, with its seventy-year tableau of the life of Port William's bachelor barber and of the twentieth century's vast alterations in rural life. If Jayber becomes something of an unofficial historian within the narratives of Port William, there is another important narrator at work in the fiction. A few of the smaller novels pick up threads of the life of Andy Catlett, the figure who seems to serve as Berry's own persona throughout the fiction—born in 1934, the same year as Berry; raised by both a lawyer father in town and by farmer grandparents, like Berry; leaving the farm to pursue a more cosmopolitan life as a writer, Andy as a journalist and Berry as a novelist; then returning to the farm, to his roots, to the land and people for whom he becomes a storyteller. Andy's journey back is captured in the novel *Remembering* just as Berry revisits his own return in several essays and poems. Interlaced through the narrative history are the short stories, many of them told, or rather retold, by Andy as he has culled them from his forebears, filling in nuances of the world of the Coulters and the Feltners, two families whose names are passing away at the close of the twentieth century but who live on in the faint possibilities hinted at in the novel *Hannah Coulter*. In all of Berry's fiction, the question whether local community can sustain life and health, can endure the "slings and arrows of outrageous fortune" arrayed against it, especially since World War II, is never far from the surface. At times, the only conceivable answer seems to be *"no!"* And yet there is no surrender, not as long as stories can be told and human character thus shaped and restored. At the root of this hope is the enduring practice of hospitality.

But hospitality is a tricky thing, because it has to be particularized, and it must be both offered and received; it is fully realized only when reciprocated. Thus, hospitality must be offered within the confines of a local community, or a household, or an interpersonal relationship. And more than a mere opening in the boundary is needed; there must be the creation of a safe and open space, a located offer and a located response, mingling vulnerability and responsibility. Berry's fiction provides several different portrayals of hospitality, but the degree of healing depends on the fragile dynamic that occurs at the permeable boundaries, both physical and spiritual.

Under the broad rubric of hospitality, at least six different categories of interaction seem to be represented in Berry's world. We should probably cite a prior category, or rather precategory, of those who have lived and thrived within the community and who are the initiators of much of the hospitality that is offered. These folk are not without relational tensions, but they are those, like Mat Feltner, who have lived within the gift of the local community their entire lives and most easily know how to offer it again. This category could be posited as the first principle for hospitality, a sort of "sustainable hospitality" rooted all the way back to creation.

Among the more challenging opportunities for hospitality, the first category is perhaps the closest to the classical notion of hospitality: that offered to the unknown stranger who has crossed the boundary into the community, if only briefly. Berry's fiction provides a few very moving accounts of such kindness. The second category involves those who enter into the community for a time, living and working in proximity to the "members" but never developing a devotion to place and people. These characters come and go, drifting in and out through the boundaries, usually in search of the elusive "good life" or just plain "good times." The third and fourth categories include those who grow up in Port William but abandon the possibilities laid before them (several shades of the "prodigal") and those who come from the outside but stay and are fully reckoned as "members," Jayber Crow being chief among these and also Hannah Coulter, both of whom narrate novels for Berry. A fifth group are those within the community who violate and damage relationships but then seek and/or find reconciliation; here the resiliency of the community, its ability to absorb betrayal, is tested. A final group, most intriguing and perhaps most significant to the health of the "membership," includes those who are fully a part of the community and yet who dwell, at times and in various ways, on the boundaries. The two prime examples, similar and yet quite different in their patterns, are Burley Coulter and Wheeler Catlett, central figures in much of Berry's narrative world. These character and situational variations on the theme of hospitality will hopefully reveal the tremendous challenges that confront life in the healing community. Such a community is no static world, no Shangri-La, no codified set of estates, but rather a living organism, flawed and finite but offering the healing spaces that make hope at least possible.

One note further regarding the centrality of the fictional universe here: this suggests the powerful role of narrative in creating and sustaining hospitality. The world of Port William is a world of individual stories woven together into relationships, which sometimes unravel, so that the tapestry of the "membership of Port William" has holes in it and is always frayed and repaired around the edges. But the tapestry's wealth of individual designs creates its beauty and desirability—it is the furthest thing from a generic, industrial carpet. It is sustainable only in its uniqueness and particularity, and it can fall apart within a generation (as is prophesied in both *Jayber Crow* and *Hannah Coulter*) if the healing act of weaving and repairing is not carried on. Put another way, if the stories are forgotten and there is no context—past, present, or future—then there is no identity, just an unraveled set of threads.

### Tend to the Stranger among You

The first category of hospitality, gifting the stranger with unrequested and unrequited charity, recurs throughout Berry's work. Probably the most classic example of hospitality in all of his fiction occurs in the story "The Solemn Boy," where the genial farmer Tol Proudfoot and his wife, Miss Minnie, take in a drifter and his son who walk by their farm on a cold day during the Depression. The encounter lasts only a few hours, the strangers are never named, and they leave into the dying afternoon with only an extra coat on the boy's back, but what happens at lunch is a beautiful example of a restorative, risky hospitality. When Tol and Minnie notice that the famished strangers will not or cannot communicate beyond glum monosyllables, they offer food and pleasantries in an attempt to forge some connection. Tol is especially moved by the boy's stolid silence, and after traditional jokes fall flat, he pours his buttermilk down the front of his own shirt in a kind of slapstick vulnerability. Both Tol and Minnie are amazed at what he's just done: "And then they heard the boy. At first he sounded like he had an obstruction in his throat that he worked at with a sort of strangling. And then he laughed. He laughed with a free, strong laugh that seemed to open his throat as wide as a stovepipe. It was the laugh of a boy who was completely tickled. It transformed everything."[3] The success here is real, the hospitality succeeds, but it is only a fleeting healing, a balm for the traveler who will then move on. The father and son leave with a seed planted in them, but we have no idea, and perhaps not much hope, that it will flourish.

In another story set in the earliest years of the Port William chronology, Berry portrays an incident from the childhood of Mat Feltner, the man who serves as the patriarch of the "membership" throughout the middle of the twentieth century. In "The Hurt Man," Mat is but five years old, and the events of the story make a foundational impression upon him. Into the eternality of his child's vision of life—"the world, as he knew it, simply existed, familiar even in its changes: the town, the farms, the slopes and ridges, the woods, the river, and the sky over it all"[4]—break the violence and mortality of even such a world. After a scuffle in the street of Port William on a Saturday afternoon, a wounded man comes running into the Feltners' home, and Mat's mother, having stopped the throng of onlookers in their tracks to make sure they are friend and not foe, goes to work:

3. TDL, 192.
4. Ibid., 5.

She began gently to wash his face. Wherever he was bleeding, she washed away the blood: first his face, and then his arms, and then his chest and sides. . . . What [Mat] saw in her face would remain with him forever. It was pity, but it was more than that. It was hurt love that seemed to include entirely the hurt man. . . . Mat was familiar with her tenderness and had thought nothing of it. But now he recognized it in her face and in her hands as they went out to the hurt man's wounds. To him, then, it was as though she leaned in the black of her mourning over the whole hurt world itself, touching its wounds with her tenderness, in her sorrow.[5]

The allusion to the mourning garb of Mrs. Feltner, who we find out in "Pray without Ceasing" has "borne four children and raised one"[6] and so already knows much of loss and grief, tells us something of the mutualism, the vulnerability, necessary for hospitality to thrive. That the wounded man is nameless and a stranger is insignificant. Suffering cries out of need. The analogy of the Good Samaritan does not make the story trite but deepens it.

## Just Passing Through

Among the characters in the second category, those who drift in and out through the permeable boundary of community, taking what they want (which is never relational) and leaving without warning or apparent regret, a vivid example is the hired man in *The Memory of Old Jack*, Lightning Berlew. Mat Feltner has been forced to hire help after the death of an elderly black man, Dick Watson, who had spent his whole life working for the Feltners, more friend than employee. In the crisis and lack of available men, "the worst, or near it, was what he finally got: a couple Wheeler Catlett had only heard of, this Lightning and his wife, Sylvania—known, Mat later learned, as Smoothbore. . . . 'Tell me niggers been living here,' Lightning said engagingly to Mat as he untied the mattress from

5. Ibid., 9–10.
6. Ibid., 62.

the car roof. 'If it doesn't suit you,' Mat said, 'that'll be just fine.' And that was when he learned the first principle of Lightning's character: there is no earthly way to insult him. 'Well,' Lightning said, 'that ain't nothing a little warshing won't take care of.'"[7] Further on in the narrative, as Lightning cleans up with the other workers prior to lunch, we see that "there is an arrogance in his eye and jaw and the line of his mouth, based not upon any excellence of his own but upon his contempt for excellence: if he is not the best man in the field, then he is nevertheless equal to the best man by the perfection of his scorn, for the best man and for the possibility that is incarnate in him."[8] Though space in the field and at the table has been provided for Lightning, his rejection of the gift is proof that proximity is not enough; one must not only enter the healing space of hospitality but also have the humility to see it as a gift.

One final description from the novel reveals the inability of the Berlews to feel at home within boundaries of place and community. This time the scene is the aftermath of Old Jack's death and the wake at the Feltner home. Mat is looking for a moment's rest after his vigil, but Lightning pulls up in his car and commences to repair it with Mat's tools, his wife restless to go out on the town: "This is the Berlews' evening ritual. Mat should have foreseen it. He might as well have gone to sit in the road. The Berlews are travelers; when they are not going they are getting ready to go. That is the way they will be. In acknowledging that, Mat knows he has come to a limit he has grown too old to assail. But it troubles him. He lets it trouble him."[9] The transience built into the global system touches actual human lives, uproots them, and leaves them forever rootless. Despite the mutual need—Mat needs a laborer, the Berlews need an income—and despite the reality of the Feltners' hospitality—they would never stoop to condescension—there is a clear failure in this dynamic, and the aftermath is merely tolerance.

7. MOJ, 11.
8. Ibid., 83.
9. Ibid., 156.

## Various Shades of the Prodigal

The third category where hospitality is at stake is the tenuous exchange by which children of Port William choose whether to partake of the "membership" offered them, not just by blood and proximity but by love and commitment. Because this is a healing community, it is not insular; people are free to come and go, and some of the reasons, such as the military draft or going off to college, are shown to be part of the confusion of obligations. The question here is, once a person is pulled across the boundary and "sees the world," how will he or she respond to the offer of renewed finitude? In the final excerpt from *The Memory of Old Jack* offered above, we see the drifting Berlews critiqued by a weary Mat Feltner. The second half of the critique that Mat ponders there involves a deeper breach, a breach of trust and faithfulness and kinship by a familiar culprit, Old Jack's daughter Clara, who has left behind the close boundaries of Port William for a comfortable life in Louisville with her banker husband, Glad Pettit. Clara has returned for her father's funeral and turned it into her own statement of difference and superiority, outfitting her father's corpse with an opulence he eschewed in life: "For the coffin testified to its costliness with the assertive elegance of the Pettits' automobile—a veritable Cadillac of a coffin. Its sedately burnished lid opened upon a spotless drift of white as deep and soft as a summer cloud. Upon the cumulus of eternal ease, Old Jack lay in a dark, richly woven suit, a white shirt and a tie. The face raised upon the satin pillow had been stuffed and smoothed to look not as Old Jack had ever looked."[10] Such a displacement had been brewing a long time, ever since Jack and Ruth had labored away amidst marital strife and infidelity to send Clara to a finishing school, only to see her meet Glad and forever displace herself from the country. Jack had made one last attempt, in his own old age and with Ruth dead and buried, to reconnect by trying to persuade Glad and Clara to buy an adjoining farm and retire out to Port William with him: "if his own daughter could only

10. Ibid., 153–54.

take some comfort from and give some care to the place that he had served all his life, then that would be enough."[11] After Glad's patronizing response, Jack finally sees that the attempt to relocate his daughter and son-in-law within the circle of affection is vain: "As had come to be his way, he merely accepted that his daughter and son-in-law were of a kind that was estranged and alien, and probably inimical, to his kind. A man without a place that he respects, he thought, may do *anything* with money."[12]

What emerges from Jack's death and the eventual auctioning of his land by Clara and Glad is a further sign of the severing that comes when the community is left behind, not just in proximity but in spirit. In the short story "It Wasn't Me," which we saw in chapter 6 as the moment of Elton Penn's full adoption into the membership, there is also a dark side of the narrative, involving the Pettits. When Jack left a sketchy message giving Elton half the buying price and naming him as the desired buyer, Wheeler assumed this would be sufficient. But "he had done his assuming, as he often did, in a world that he assumed was ruled by instinctive decency. That Clara and Glad Pettit did not inhabit that particular world, they let him know fast."[13] As Wheeler begins to hatch his scheme for helping Elton buy the land regardless of meddling and cost, he reflects on the distance Clara has gone from the membership:

> As he watches her, it seems to Wheeler that she is elated, and he realizes with the sudden astonishment that one feels in looking into a life beyond the possibilities of one's own, that for her the sale of the farm is a freedom, her own connection with it, her own early life there, being merely an encumbrance, probably an embarrassment. . . . How much better it would be to be at peace with them, fellow mortals as they are, kindred as they are. And yet he feels, as he knows Old Jack felt, the irreconcilable division between his kind and their kind, between the things of this world and their value in money.[14]

11. Ibid., 137.
12. Ibid., 138.
13. TDL, 268–69.
14. Ibid., 277.

151

What Wheeler lays out here seems to be the boundary-land between the bounded life and the "American dream," and rather than seeing the two as a progression, he sees them as utterly at odds. There is a whole new "mind" that evolves when things become merely commodities, and no amount of appeal to loyalty and kinship can undo that damage. Once the Pettits have reduced their considerations of place and people to property values, the space of hospitality is squeezed down close to disappearance.

In contrast, there are characters for whom the damage of departure can be assuaged only by a return to the community and by finding their place once again. This is true of Art Rowanberry, who goes off from the family farm into an artillery brigade in World War II Europe. The story "Making It Home" is set during Art's homecoming, but most of the narrative focuses on a solitary and haunted ten-mile walk from the bus station on the Ohio River to the family farm in Port William. Art has been wounded, not just in body but in spirit, and he doesn't know if he can conceive of wholeness again:

> The fighting went on, the great tearing apart. People and everything else were torn into pieces. Everything was only pieces put together that were ready to fly apart, and nothing was whole. You got to where you could not look at a man without knowing how little it would take to kill him. For a man was nothing but just a little morsel of soft flesh and brittle bone inside of some clothes. And you could not look at a house or a schoolhouse or a church without knowing how, rightly hit, it would shake down into a pile of stones and ashes. There was nothing you could look at that was whole—man or beast or house or tree—that had the right to stay whole very long.[15]

Art becomes anxious that he cannot fully return home, or cannot return wholly, as he reflects: "I am not a stranger, but I am changed. Now I know a mighty power that can pass over the earth and make it strange. There are people, where I have been, that won't know

15. Ibid., 224.

their places when they get back to them. Them that live to get back won't be where they were when they left."[16]

Out of this unhealthy experience of war's violence, when boundaries are forced and coerced, Art crosses back into the healing finitude. He approaches the hillside of his family's farm anxiously—and his father sees him and says only "Well now!" and younger brother Mart asks, "You reckon your foot'll still fit in a furrow?"[17] That invitation back to the land, the earth, and the hearth and all that his family and home represents is balm for Art's wounds. It seems once again not only to evoke but to enrich the "prodigal son" narrative for the elder Mr. Rowanberry to end the story by telling the young nephew, "Honey, run yonder to the house. Tell your granny to set on another plate. For we have our own that was gone and has come again."[18] Here is the restored "place at the table," the coming again into full communion through hospitality, that can heal the worst that a man has witnessed.[19]

## Come and Stay Awhile

The permeability of the membership's boundaries also allows for "strangers and aliens" to come within the healing space and to dwell, without strings and with full acceptance as "members." This is our fourth category, and Berry seems to have found this particular trope on hospitality to be intriguing in recent years, as the narrators of two of his later novels, *Jayber Crow* and *Hannah Coulter*, both fit this description more or less. Jayber, though born in Port William, is orphaned as a small child, tended at the outskirts of the community for a time by surrogate parents, and then sent off to an orphanage followed by a Bible college, before his return as a grown man and "stranger" in the unlikely role of town barber.

16. Ibid., 232.
17. Ibid., 235.
18. Ibid., 236.
19. See also the novel *Remembering*, where Berry seems to subtly trace his own departure and return to the farm, his own disorientation and reconciliation, through the journey of Andy Catlett away from the "membership," into success and illusion and thence disillusion, and then back to the farm, where the damages must be faced.

For Jayber, reception back into the community is a long and uneven affair (never accomplished, as far as many of the women of the town are concerned!). But at the crucial moment of his return, in the midst of the worse flood in memory, the hospitality of Burley Coulter and Mat Feltner offers him the first step in. Burley's Charon-like ferrying of Jayber to safety through the flood we have mentioned earlier, but it is Burley's paternal interest in Jayber's taking over the recently abandoned Port William barbershop that opens the door of hospitality:

> After he had thought, he said, "Well, well. I remember you. I sure do. And what's your line of work, Mr. Crow?"
>
> "I'm a barber."
>
> He had a further thought, then, that amused him. "Now, I reckon you work in one of them big fancy shops –in Louisville, I imagine— with fans in the ceiling and a shoeshine stand and a pretty woman that files fingernails."
>
> "Not hardly," I said. "At present, I'm out of a job."
>
> "Well, now! Ain't that a coincident! Or did you know? They're fresh out of a barber at Port William."[20]

Burley eventually takes Jayber to see the ramshackle shop/apartment and shows it off like an excitable realtor:

> "Yessir!" Burley said, seeing a vision. "Why, a single man with a place like this would be *fixed*. He'd have his dwelling place and his place of business right together." . . .
>
> It was clear that he wanted me to buy the shop, but at the time I had no idea of his reason. Had he bought the shop himself from Barber Horsefield, and was wanting to sell it at a profit? Was he anxious to redeem his own vision of the good life a man could live in such a place? Or, maybe, did he like me?
>
> I hoped so . . .[21]

This hopefulness in the face of unexpected intimacy (or at least interest, of which Jayber had known little in his life) is encouraged

20. JC, 91–92.
21. Ibid., 99–100.

when Burley takes Jayber to bargain with Mat Feltner, who, as bank trustee, controls the mortgage. Mat is a key figure in Berry's fiction, the link in the membership between the old and the new; his character is no-nonsense, and his hospitality sober and earnest:

> Mr. Feltner—who would not be "Mat" to me for a long time—turned to me and stuck out his hand. "Mr. Crow, I'm Mat Feltner. I'm glad to know you. I knew your mother's people. I remember the Daggets very well."
>
> There was nothing glancing or sidling about the way he looked at you. He looked right through your eyes, right into you, as a man looks at you who is willing for you to look right into him. . . . He said, "Three hundred dollars'll buy the shop and whatever's in it. We'll need a third of the money down, the shop for collateral." He went on to set out all the terms of the loan, fair enough, but very strict in what he would expect of me.
>
> When he had finished, the room was quiet. You will appreciate the tenderness of my situation if I remind you that I had managed to live for years without being *known* to anybody. And that day two men who knew who and where I had come from had looked at me face-on, as I had not been looked at since I was a child.[22]

Jayber proves himself worthy by pulling the down payment from his jacket lining and his shoe, and he finds that he shows them more than financial solvency—he shows them that he wants to be with them, that he receives the beginnings of community. Jayber observes, "Burley Coulter and Mat Feltner proved good friends to me from the start. They didn't just get me started and then leave me to fare the best I could."[23] So here, in the literal space of the barbershop but also in the space where hospitality is extended, Jayber finds himself, if not whole, on the path to healing, to knowing what wholeness promises. The crucial point here is not that Jayber was born in Port William and so technically is at home; in fact, he is intentionally unknown and unknowable until this moment. But he will never again be without a home.

22. Ibid., 101–2.
23. Ibid, 103.

Hannah Coulter marries into the Feltner family from the outside and is widowed when Virgil Feltner goes missing during in World War II and is presumed dead, whereupon she becomes an adopted daughter of the family. Her subsequent marriage to Nathan Coulter further cements her place in the community—but it is not just marital status that brings her in. The offering and receiving of hospitality in painful times, often a leap of faith without clear ends or goals, is part of the pattern that weaves Hannah in. When Hannah enters the narrative world of Port William in the novel *A Place on Earth*, she is very much a "beautiful stranger" though from a town only a few miles away. Her courtship with Virgil involves a sort of probing and testing, since no one knows her family, and even after she marries him and enters the core of the "membership" in the Feltner household,[24] his departure for the war, from which he never returns, leaves her a young widowed mother in a place where she doesn't quite belong. Yet as one follows her subsequent courtship with Nathan Coulter after his return from the war and her seeking of consent from the Feltners as her "adoptive" parents, one sees the strands of kinship are more tightly woven than they appeared.

Relative to Jayber Crow's signature moment of acceptance, Hannah's entry into the hospitable space of community has been more gradual, more fragile. But when we see her helping the aged Jack Beechum to dinner in *The Memory of Old Jack*, after a few years of marriage and work and childbearing with Nathan, there is a sense not only of the healing she's experienced but of her full place in the community of which Old Jack is patriarch:

> In his gaze she feels herself to be not just physically but historically a woman, one among generations, bearing into the mystery the dark seed. She feels herself completed by that as she could not be completed by the desire of a younger man. . . . She is moved by him, pleased to stand in his sight, whose final knowledge is womanly, who knows that all human labor passes into mystery, who has been faithful unto death

---

24. Hannah articulates this acceptance as something not just familial but communal: "I was making myself at home. . . . I had come unknowing into what Burley would have called the 'membership' of my life. I was becoming a member of Port William" (HC, 42).

to the life of his fields to no end that he will know in this world. As for Old Jack, he listens to the sound of her voice, strong and full of hope, knowing and near to joy, that pleases him and tells him what he wants to know. He nods and smiles, encouraging her to go on. Occasionally he praises her, in that tone of final judgment old age has given him, "You're a fine woman. You're all right," he says. And his tone implies: Believe it of yourself forever.[25]

So Hannah the widow, like Jayber the orphan, has found her place, or rather has been found and placed by one of the keepers of the story. Eventually both Hannah and Jayber become storytellers for the membership, and though their tales are darkened by tragedy, they are continuations of the long story and hence continuations of hope. By the end of *Hannah Coulter* the novel, Hannah's story is in danger of being lost by the ravages of community at the start of the early twenty-first century. And yet at her doorstep in the end is another stranger, her own grandson Virgie Settlemeyer, a drifting twenty-something such as could appear in any of our lives, but he has at least arrived at the threshold, the possibility, of home. Hannah can only extend her hospitality and make that vulnerable space, but if that is the only mechanism for Virgie's healing, we have seen in Berry's fiction how powerful it can be. As Hannah herself states: "Some day, maybe in a year or so, we will begin to know what this amounts to. After drugs and escape and whatever freedom he has tried, can he stand what has got to be stood?"[26] We have cause to grieve, and maybe cause to hope.

## Internal Wounds

One of the sharpest tests of hospitality comes when there is betrayal and wounding from within the boundaries, from among one's own. Such is the case in the story "Pray without Ceasing," set in 1912 for the most part, though framed with Andy Catlett pondering

25. MOJ, 81.
26. HC, 184.

decades later the strange confluence of lines that met in his grand-fathers. The story relates the murder of Ben Feltner, Mat's father and Andy's great-grandfather, by a cousin and friend, Thad Coulter, who had fallen into a drunken despondency and was offended by Ben's rebuke. As the story unfolds, the relationship of both blood and friendship between the killer and the killed keeps arising to be reckoned with. According to a yellowed newspaper report that Andy receives from an old neighbor, "[Ben's] assailant, Thad Coulter, had said, upon turning himself in to the sheriff at Hargrave soon after the incident, 'I've killed the best friend I ever had.' "[27] Mat's rage, Jack Beechum's stemming of his nephew's rage, and the adjustment of Ben's family to the shocking news are recounted—and then there is Thad's daughter, Martha Elizabeth. Having unsuccessfully tried to stop her father's reckless deed, she follows him after the murder, hoping to guide him back to sense. Her pursuit guides Thad to the sheriff's office, where Thad, upon sobering, cannot see her without succumbing to his guilt and shame. Yet as Andy's grandmother tells him years later, it is Martha Elizabeth's love that overcomes the brokenness her father had wrought upon the community and himself: "But in the same moment he saw his guilt included in love that stood as near him as Martha Elizabeth and at that moment wore her flesh. It was surely weak and wrong of him to kill himself—to sit in judgment that way over himself. But surely God's love includes people who can't bear it. . . . If God loves the ones we can't . . . then finally maybe we can."[28]

That this love can be channeled from God through people who are kin is amazing enough; that the community as a whole can absorb such wounds and love in like degree betokens the miraculous scope of hospitality. Andy's final reflection on the story, the web of which has caught him in all its various strands, shows the depth of healing possible: "I am blood kin to both sides of that moment when Ben Feltner turned to face Thad Coulter in the road and Thad pulled the trigger. The two families, sundered in the ruin of a friendship,

27. TDL, 41.
28. Ibid., 69–70.

were united again first in new friendship and then in marriage. My grandfather made peace here that has joined many who would otherwise have been divided. I am the child of his forgiveness."[29] In the face of brokenness, the offer of hospitality can still be extended, not just after the boundaries are realigned but as a way of fundamentally establishing them. Forgiveness becomes a way of distinguishing between self and other and allowing the space of hospitality to exist once again. We mustn't lose sight of how risky such extension of hospitality is, in the wake of violence and in the face of violence's constant possibility. But the fruit is revealed in a story like this, when the life-giving power of community is tested and tests true.[30]

## Membership at the Margins

Our final variant on this theme of hospitality is in some ways the most elusive. Two of the crucial characters in the "membership of Port William" are Burley Coulter and Wheeler Catlett, men whose lives are woven deeply into the healing community but who, at the same time and in different ways, don't quite fit. Each dwells at the margins of the farm and the land, attached but not wholly so. This is where hospitality, as the vulnerable and permeable boundary of love, shows a unique sort of payback for the risk. A richer health is fostered for the community by the quirky roles and temperaments allowed to flourish in such figures as Burley or Wheeler.

Burley is the free spirit of the "membership," the convivial joker and reveler who can also turn into a solitary woodsman, the hardworking farmer who never really wants to own a farm, the casual lover who tends and fathers his illegitimate son faithfully. He is a contradiction that threatens to break and fracture the healing bonds of the community—yet he never does. Perhaps it is that he sustains

29. Ibid., 75.

30. Another story from *That Distant Land* that points to this willingness of the community to tend its vulnerable people is "Watch with Me." This narrative of a group of farmers, led by Tol Proudfoot, following a mentally ill neighbor, Nightlife Hample, through the woods and gullies for a day and a half as he wanders in a daze carrying Tol's loaded shotgun, is full of humor and pathos and, ultimately, love.

the "spirit of the law" of community, of natural affections for land and people, even though he never quite follows the "letter of the law." Within the boundaries there needs to be space even for particularity that threatens those boundaries or takes a unique approach to them. Burley refuses to be controlled by some simple set of expectations, yet, in a way, no one is more faithful to the community.

From the earliest references to Burley in the chronology of the fiction, his reputation of pressing margins is presented. When Tol Proudfoot attends the schoolhouse Harvest Festival to attempt a courtship with the teacher, Miss Minnie, one of the performances he witnesses is that of the young Burley Coulter butchering the poem "When the Frost Is on the Punkin'" by James Whitcomb Riley. Despite Miss Minnie's valiant efforts at prompting,

> she looked up to see an expression on his face that she knew too well. The blush was gone; he was grinning; the light of inspiration was in his eyes.
>
> "Well, drot it, folks," he said, "I forgot her. But I'll tell you one I *heard*."
>
> Miss Minnie rose, smiling, and said in a tone of utter gratification, "*Thank* you, Burley! Now you may be seated."[31]

That reputation for mischief stays with Burley through various twists and turns. He and his father Dave are present a few years later chatting in the street of Port William with Ben Feltner at the moment Ben is shot and killed, as described in "Pray without Ceasing." Here Burley has been introduced briefly: "Except for his boyish face and grin, Burley was a grown man. He was seventeen, a square-handed, muscular fellow already known for the funny things he said, though his elders knew of them only by hearsay."[32] A few years further on, in the story "Watch with Me," Tol Proudfoot and his entourage meet Burley in the woods, where he sneaks up on Put Woolfork in the dark and pokes him in the back, creating a stir for which Tol rebukes his boyishness: "Burley was twenty-one that year, old enough to take

31. TDL, 34.
32. Ibid., 54.

160

the word *boy* either as a judgment or as a pleasantry. Tol offered it as both, and Burley received it with his grin unaltered."[33]

Here, the hint of Burley's wildness—he has been in the woods for two days, ostensibly chasing a runaway hound—suggests a pattern that an aged Burley himself characterizes, in the story "The Wild Birds," as "wayward."[34] "The Wild Birds" tells of the great divide between Burley and Wheeler yet also the powerful bonds that unite them. Both are old men when Burley comes to Wheeler's law office. In this story Wheeler's "equal and opposite" marginalization is evident. Wheeler could be a threatening figure for the health of the community, given that he has gone away to college and law school and now lives in the county seat of Hargrave, where he might well have become a junior version of a Glad Pettit. His life, however, has been dedicated to the farmers and the country folk, and most of his off-hours are spent driving among the farms of Port William in his muddy and scratched Buick, as he seeks to keep his finger upon the pulse of the people and places he loves.

Burley is in Wheeler's office to alter his last will and testament. He wants to leave the old Coulter place to his illegitimate son, Danny Branch, as an act of natural justice. But he's gone about his life wildly, and he knows this is painful to Wheeler. It is Burley's willingness to confess and to make right (though he knows he can never make real restitution to Kate Helen Branch, his lover and Danny's mother, who died long ago), that shows how deeply he understands the "membership" of which he has been a wayward part.

When Wheeler stares down Burley in his law office in 1967, it is the continuity and health of the membership that he has on his mind, but whereas Burley has been too loose at times, Wheeler tends to be too tight, too caught up in the details. If Burley is the wild topsoil, then Wheeler is the human ordering. He wants to preserve the community, all its fragility and vulnerability, by force of planning and legal prudence. But things are more organic, as he well knows. Ten years later, in the story "Fidelity," we find Wheeler going toe to toe with a state

33. Ibid., 106.
34. Ibid., 350.

161

police detective sent to investigate the "abduction" of Burley from the intensive-care unit of a hospital in Louisville. Danny Branch is the key suspect, and the breaches of propriety afoot should be of the sort to torment the aged (but decidedly unretired) Wheeler. Yet his diatribe to Detective Bode reveals that perhaps he has more in common with Burley's natural affections than he does with the letter of the law. Countering Bode's charge that Danny may have acted out of greed, killing off his father for inheritance money, Wheeler responds roundly:

> So there certainly is room for greed and mercy of another kind. I don't doubt that Danny, assuming he is the guilty party, has considered the cost; he's an intelligent man. Even so, I venture to say to you that you're wrong about him, insofar as you suspect him of acting out of greed. I'll give you two reasons that you had better consider. In the first place, he loves Burley. In the second place, he's not alone, and he knows it. You're thinking of a world in which the legatee stands all alone, facing a legator who has now become a mere obstruction between legatee and legacy. But you have thought up the wrong world. There are several of us here who belong to Danny and to whom he belongs, and we'll stand by him, whatever happens. After money, you know, we are talking about the question of the ownership of people. To whom and to what does Burley Coulter belong? If, as you allege, Danny Branch has taken Burley Coulter out of the hospital, he has done it because Burley belongs to him.[35]

If we follow Wheeler's lead (and the detective eventually does, in spite of himself), then we can see community through a whole new lens, that of mutual ownership, not in economic terms, but in terms of hospitality, of selves and households connecting to become fully human. The space that is made for such connecting thus belongs to no one and to everyone.

All these nuances and variations reveal that Berry's fictional world is far from romantic; most of the stories take up some violence or violation of boundaries, some tension in the fabric of community.

35. Ibid., 417.

Nevertheless, hospitality is possible, its attempt essential to the health and healing of the local community, even in a broken, fractured, disordered world. Each of the categories that we've elaborated upon above provides unique chances and risks. Strangers come and go, as we have seen, sometimes cordially and sometimes selfishly. Our own children, friends, and neighbors sometimes leave us behind and trade their world of relationship for a world of illusions and alternative promises. But we have known strangers who have become part of the web of our lives; perhaps we ourselves have been in that role, like Jayber Crow, looking for a home and actually finding it. All of us have faced hurt and betrayal and have had to confront the hard choices that reconciliation requires. We've all been challenged and frustrated by those who travel the boundaries differently than ourselves. If hospitality is the answer in each of these cases, through offers of love and space and possibility, however risky, then one of our prime questions in life must be "How do we extend our hands and hearts in hospitality?" Without such extension, community cannot offer healing and character can never be developed.

So at the boundaries of the community, as at the center (with a figure like Mat Feltner), and at the vectors that pierce through or spiral in and out, healing is possible because hospitality has room for the wounded (and for being wounded). The finite community thus shows an almost infinite array of ways to love, to forgive, to keep, and even to give away. There truly is room for everyone, with the only caveat being that love must be accepted as given; it must be received as gift.

# 9

············

# Bounded Hope in the Household and House of God

Having followed Berry's ideas this far, we want to extend the conversation to two institutions that we're particularly interested in: the church and the realm of education. If you've read this far, you'll not be surprised that Berry is hard on both entities, citing both for contributing to the dissolution of communities. His essays on the church's role in the misuse of creation and of higher education's role in promoting the corporate mind and the dislocated society we live in have opened up for us the alarming reality that these structures that we live and work and fellowship within are too often part of the slide toward the inhospitable, unhealthy, posthuman world that looms like a specter.

Yet we are strangely hopeful, not in spite of Berry's critique (and hopefully not just because we are comfortable in our churches and make our living in higher education), but rather because of the alternative world, the hope of hospitality, that Berry has revealed fully to us. That hope motivates us now to devote these final two chapters to these places of deep concern, places marked by disease, but whose potential role in fostering real health needs to be vigorously championed.

We've come to see Berry's measure of life in "bounded hope" as a helpful curb on the possible dangers of a vision of "all of life as redeemable," a phrase born of Reformed worldview discourse and played out even in evangelical apologies for worldview, social justice, and cultural engagement. While we don't doubt that all of creation will be redeemed eschatologically when Christ comes to rule and reign over his Kingdom without end, such a hope is misappropriated when it is used as a charge for the Christian community to either coerce the Kingdom into place or simply replicate pop culture without real directional change. In both cases there is no recognition of boundedness, so that energies and resources leak out in a thousand different directions. If redemption is to happen in a fallen world, a world of limited resources, then difficult choices must be made as we invest ourselves and our lives into the critical junctures of God's Kingdom. We argue, following Berry, that the priority of the local is at least a helpful starting place in guiding these decisions.

What seems a considerably skeptical, even crotchety, vision of culture in Berry's work has a realizable and effectual mooring in his emphasis on boundary, limit, and finitude as the path to healing and health. Berry points not to a grand vision or movement but to as many variations on the call as there are located communities, real people in real places with real problems. Such a view has helped us see how properly focused churches and educational institutions might be part of a solution to the fundamental "health" crisis in which not just our bodies but our very human selves hang in the balance. How many of us would be able to say that our church or our educational institution makes our community more hospitable, more human? If Berry is at all right, these institutions have too often the opposite effect; but working through the failures is a way to get at the hopeful possibilities. So we begin with the church.

## The Dislocated Church

How do we begin to embody the notions that Berry has suggested so eloquently, especially when our everyday lives, at work and at church, don't seem eloquent at all? How do we turn the corner, or rather dig in our heels, against the pull of a "posthuman" magnetism that seems to have our culture in its grip? This is a critical question for our time, perhaps *the* critical question from a Berryian point of view, since the "posthuman" revalues people by function and instrumentality instead of creational worth. Furthermore, inevitable progress toward maximized value is a norm that allows us to avoid problems by faulty advances and leaps across boundaries. Rural folks can escape the problems of the country by a move to the suburbs, troubled marriages can be "remedied" by divorce and dislocation of family fragments, residents in faltering school systems can opt out their own children and forget the plight of their neighbors, and behind the veil of supply and demand we can dislocate our economic choices even in the neighborhood grocery chain. Even the church in the Western world has not escaped these deep influences, since it has become a place to maximize one's own valuation, even at the expense of displacement and failure to develop community and hence character. The generic megachurch, like the generic supermarket, the generic unified school district, the generic local political party apparatus, is actually the perverse byproduct of a reduced human-ity. In every aspect of life, we are left with only the "bingo game" of comparison shopping and brand loyalties, whether of worship service, bottled water, or county commissioner.

We recognize that not every instance of disease can be remedied in this life—the ravages are simply too severe. There are marriages where irreparable harm has been done, churches that have disintegrated and need to be abandoned, neighborhoods that are no longer livable— but these are the cussed exceptions that show the severity of human misdirection, and they should cause us to grit our teeth not only in anguish but in determination to change what we can. Here we seek to undermine the culture of mobility while also resisting the judgmental stance offered by homogenous "solutions." I (Matt) have seen the failure of standardized zoning codes to stem the tide of suburban sprawl and to reckon with quality-of-life issues outside the realm of convenience and value. Indeed, my experience on our township's

167

planning commission has revealed the panoply of loopholes hidden deep within every set of rules, waiting for exploitation.

Our first turn is to the church, because it seems intended by God precisely to be the place where, through acts of communal worship, fellowship, and confession, we most consciously avoid dehumanizing ourselves and others. We don't want to, indeed cannot, speak as external critics; it is precisely our involvement in our two particular churches that makes this critique and this hopefulness urgent. Our two churches are very different in style and approach, and neither would be highlighted in any discussion of avant-garde trends within ecclesiology. We offer no new program, no call to revolution, no steps, per se, to revival; we are simply tracing a path toward health.

Redemptive work within creation has to be located, so as finite beings we have to make hard decisions: where does healing need to start? We have posited the local church, but Berry immediately forces us to revisit that seemingly automatic choice. His critique of the church, that its concerns have tended to remove it to the margins of communal life, alien to the place where it resides, is both troubling and helpful. In a way, the church has owned this criticism by seeking solutions through insular practices. Now, if the local church should be a group of people committed to a particular community in a particular place, then questions of church "success" should never be asked without reference to place. Likewise, the more dislocated a church becomes, the more abstract and idealized its message becomes. All the good intention behind programs ends up evaporating when there is no adjustment to the people and place where the church finds itself. Berry often differentiates between a house—the replicable structure in which any people might dwell—and a home, the specific place where a specific family lives its specific story. If we stretch that distinction to ecclesiology, we might suggest a similar divide between the church "called out" of a given place and into a set of programs and patterns that are easily importable and exportable, and the church "called to be with" a given place and its inhabitants. In the latter instance, the worshiping community is called to listen to God's Word alongside the cries and needs of the community to which it is called.

So we're left with (or perhaps begin with) a series of tough questions: Should church growth, programs that attract crowds, a balanced budget, and an efficient professional staff become ends unto themselves, absolute criteria for health—or might they be a mask for disease? Should it be optional whether a church factors in its neighborhood and community, with the strengths and weaknesses, environmental and economic needs, in its vision-casting? Should the church be construed as playing a privileged role in relationship to the community in which it dwells? Or more pointedly, is the church a community unto itself with its own isolated story, rather than being located in the broader story of its locale?

In his work, Berry leans heavily toward the latter conception. In his telling of the story of a community, as we have shown, he makes place central. This means that the legitimacy of both the members and their institutions involves participation within the shared life of the community. If we are following Berry's lead, the church's purposes cannot be external to the community if it is to be a vital part. In Berry's fiction, the presence of the local church in Port William is marginal, at best, to the health of the community. Characters are not formed within the walls of the church, and inasmuch as the church destabilizes the rural community by employing transient pastors on their way to bigger congregations, harm is done even in the functional roles, the "marrying and burying," that require just a modicum of pastoral connection. Hence, in the funeral debacle from *The Memory of Old Jack*, the young minister is offered counsel by Mat Feltner prior to Jack's funeral:

"We want a simple graveside service, nothing else."

That was not what Brother Wingfare had expected. Mat leaned forward, resting his elbows on his knees, and smiled at him.

"My friend," he said, "I want you to understand this." He considered for a moment and went on. "He was not a churchly man. He was a man of unconfining righteousness. He stuck with us to the end. He never liked a great deal of fussing and formality, and we don't

169

want it imposed on him now. That would be kicking him while he's down, if you know what I mean."[1]

Mat's gravity in this situation seems to affect the novice preacher, who never even met Old Jack, but then Jack's consummately unlikable daughter Clara arrives, with a great show of money and falsified kinship, and she persuades the minister to offer a lengthy, windy prayer over an opulently coffined and outfitted corpse. Mat meets this utter failure of propriety with one of Berry's greatest images of dissent, as, in the midst of the exhortational prayer, he "exercises for the first time his prerogative as the oldest man. He turns his back and gazes upon his fields."[2]

Mat's gesture, beautiful in its context, nevertheless symbolizes an all too tempting choice for us today—how can we keep from turning our backs on a church that speaks too much and says not enough, a church that seems to know everything about the global reach of the gospel but nothing about the people within its own embrace? In trying to redeem all of life, to create programs that are all inclusive, to stretch beyond the subtle boundaries of place and person, the modern church imperils those very real human beings who need the humanness of the body of Christ more than its relevance. We want to be clear that we are not suggesting a limitation to the sweep of the Kingdom of God, nor are we trying to finagle another version of the sacred-secular divide, whereby certain spheres of life are excluded from God's redemptive presence. But in hearing Berry's voice of caution, his call for restraint and boundedness that are life-giving, we can't help but temper the triumphalism of much Christian worldview talk.

Despite all the church's failures, we have caught a few hopeful glimpses. My (Matt's) church in Grand Rapids has been in the same urban location for more than a hundred years—obviously the city around it has altered radically in the past century, and many similar churches have relocated to suburban contexts, abandoning the inner

1. MOJ, 151.
2. Ibid., 159.

city from which they feel wholly alienated. But this particular church has taken strides to relocate itself, not in physical location but in ability to connect with the local context and needs. This relocation hasn't been simple or uncontroversial, but the connection to homeless missions and urban ministries, as an act of hospitality that is demanded by proximity and devotion to place, has borne fruit. Testimonies from those whose lives have literally been rescued through the church's ministry have become a part of worshipers' experience there. No formulaic program could have changed the hearts and minds of a fairly conservative, highly liturgical congregation, but a commitment to that neighborhood and its residents has done so.

But Berry would likely see such a commitment as exceptional. He sees the church as a world-rejecting religion. In his essay "Christianity and the Survival of Creation," Berry finds American Christianity culpable for "the destruction of the natural world."[3] A history of North America reveals the practice of Christians who have been and continue to be "indifferent to the rape and plunder of the world and of its traditional cultures."[4] Such an attitude is possible when the world is conceived of as a mere resource that is available to human ownership. But when it is paired with the disproportionate emphasis on otherworldliness that is often present in pietistic Christianity, the result is more like a neglectful absentee landlord than one who is tending her place through a careful stewardship. Down this slippery slope the church loses altogether the crucial notion of place and ends up, in Berry's view, exploiting creation and undermining any notion of creation as home or church as healing place.

The essay shows little patience for an institution that displaces people and turns them into restless wanderers. If it is fair to conclude that Berry's suspicions about Christianity in relationship to nature can be carried into an evaluation of the association between the local church and the local community, then we might suggest that the church that does not make its people more at home within the community in which they live would be the spiritual equivalent

3. ACP, 305.
4. Ibid., 306.

of a strip-mining corporation. On this account, it's no wonder that Berry's antagonism toward the big coal companies that laid waste to much of Kentucky has been mirrored by a lengthy hiatus from, and ambivalence toward, the local church.

Sean Michael Lucas has argued that Berry is "too hard on the church,"[5] that in his critique of the church's complicity in the modern economy and warfare, little grace is extended; the complex mixture of saint and sinner that Berry celebrates in the characters of his fiction, he himself fails to recognize in the pews of the local church. Suggesting that Berry envisions too pure of a church, Lucas makes an interesting connection when he points out that "the local church's failing is in fact the failing of the local community."[6] But his critique of Berry is open to rebuttal at least from the angle that unhealthy communities and unhealthy churches are interwoven; these aren't two different sets of people. The membership overlaps and intermingles. Also, as we have persistently argued, Berry resists the idea that there even can be a thoroughly healthy community (or church), if a definitive sense of arrival is meant by that phrase. Instead, he is aiming for provisional healing communities, "works in progress" wherein the work of humility and forgiveness opens up the community to recognize the gifts of flawed and sometimes contrary people. Just as there are no pure humans, so there are no pure communities and no pure institutions, including churches.

There's no doubt that Lucas has grounds for saying that Berry is harshly dismissive of the local church as an institution. Indeed, both Berry and Lucas see a tenuous thread connecting church and community, but through reading both we are led to see a more hopeful connection, since healing local communities seem to have the capacity to reshape unhealthy patterns and revivify unhealthy institutions. Can a church survive and thrive in an unhealthy place? The answer is clearly yes, since there are churches that are healing places in the midst of dysfunctional inner cities, fragmented suburbs,

5. Sean Michael Lucas, "God and Country: Wendell Berry's Theological Vision," *Christian Scholar's Review* 32, no. 1 (Fall 2002): 91.
6. Ibid.

and deadened rural areas. Likewise, can communities find healing without the presence of a located and connected church? This one's a little tougher and strikes right at the tension Lucas sees in Berry's work, but we'd have to say that God's grace extends in multitudinous directions and so some measure of healing can be present (and is present in Port William). Yet in both cases, at both extremities, there's always a threat of fragmentation to our humanity, if we are forced to split our allegiances and only partially heal. An inner-city church can't rectify every economic injustice, solve every sociological dysfunction, beautify every abandoned corner lot—but it can foster attentiveness to the sorrows and the possibilities to which God's people need to attend. Likewise, the hospitable and tightly woven local community, though filled with the possibility of human love and help, will be lacking in a completeness of kingdom hope without the church's presence. And, to push the conversation beyond Berry and Lucas, whenever a community attempts to exclude the church for the sake of liberalism's mythical neutrality or maybe just out of impatience and a lack of charity, there will be a shrinking of people, a shearing off of some fundamental humanness bound up in our spiritual selves.

One of the ironies of this conversation is that in the midst of thoroughgoing attempts by churches to dislocate themselves, either explicitly or implicitly, the conditions that affect the community will also affect the local church. Economic problems in a town mean a drop in giving, for example. Apathy within a church toward the practices of the state can contribute to a moral insensitivity to the plight of one's neighbor. And because, as Lucas reminds us, the local church is made up of a subset of the community's membership, there is destined to be an overlap of consequences. Ignoring the connections between church and community is another version of dislocation, one fostered by mutual anxiety and self-protection.

In William Cavanaugh's *Torture and Eucharist* we see an extreme example of what can happen when secular and sacred concerns are bifurcated. Cavanaugh's extended argument shows that the torture and murder characteristic of Pinochet's Chile reached the extent that they did because the Catholic Church of Chile came to understand its concern to be for the spiritual as disconnected from the political.[7] In this case, as well as other significant historical examples, the church's dislocation has contributed not just to inhospitable communities but to violent ones.

The church's complicity with diseased forces in both Berry's discussion of Christianity and creation, and Cavanaugh's examination of torture, does not come as a result of the church's making the community's concerns its own. There is not a fusion. Rather, the complicity develops only when the church focuses on its unique concerns. In such a case, the church may be a healing place, but that healing is difficult to translate into the life of the local community. As Berry has stated in "The Body and Earth": "Our fragmentation of the subject cannot be our cure, because it is our disease."[8] If in its practices the church displaces people from their communities, the answer cannot be to reassert the importance of the church by making it into a substitute local community. Making people "feel at home" in church can be escapist with dangerous consequences. The church must find a way to dwell with the local community, even as the community must be open to the church's presence in its midst. There must be a shared story, a layered story that's hospitable enough to invite fallen, finite dwellers to be with one another.

## Re-placing the Church

How does a local church create a story in its place which has enough weight and meaning to root it there and to give each individual a place within the story? Here the story of scripture, especially in its call to tangible justice and mercy, gives a direction for each church to build its story, and for each person within the church to

7. William Cavanaugh, *Torture and Eucharist: Theology, Politics, and the Body of Christ* (Oxford: Blackwell, 1998). We would also include the "confessing church's" comments on the dislocation of the Protestant church in Germany under Nazism, as captured in "A Theological Declaration of Barmen" (1934). Both Karl Barth and Dietrich Bonhoeffer had a hand in writing this critique.

8. ACP, 99.

locate and anchor his or her story. Instead of churches full of families and individuals with no homes and stories of their own—or only homogenous, programmatic pseudo-stories to buy into—the healing church becomes an embodied narrative.

What the community needs is for the church to be not just a replication of the tastes of the community but rather an alternative that is also familiar enough—a different set of answers to recognizable problems. It is within these tensions and paradoxes that we recognize and proffer the Berryian vision for the church. The church must be life-giving, not simply by countercultural reaction but through cultivation in time and place. Again, it is only within healthy boundaries that life can be given. The church must be radical, but with an etymological clarity, since *radix* is the Latin for "root" and hence carries that sense of place rather than wild displacement.

Ultimately, we find the whole church-culture discussion unsatisfactory if it implies (as it so often does) that both culture and church are homogenous, globalized entities without shape or place. What we are after, following upon Berry's vision for the healing local community, is the flourishing of placed and peopled churches within local cultures. Without sacrificing any of the authority, practices, and traditions of the church universal, local churches must be particularized not just accidentally and arbitrarily but as the first principle for embodiment. There is always the simple call of scripture for the church to be the church, but our understanding of boundary, finitude, and limit as life-giving possibilities turns us toward each idiosyncratic and beautifully different body of believers, within that great unity of the people of God. This is not a reinvention of church but a reassertion of its crucial connection to local community.

As we begin to envision such churches, one place to start might be the innocuous item of church nomenclature. We've all noted the disconcerting trend, possibly borrowed from subdivisions, of churches' being named for places that don't actually exist or ideals that are unembodied. This is clearly linked to a desire to become more attractive by dislocating from geographic place-names (as well as denominational markers). At first glance, New Life Fellowship

Community Church (we have no particular assembly in mind here!) seems like a more vigorous name than Maple Street Christian Church. But what might the specificity of a tangible place in the name of a church suggest? Could the idea be reinvigorated, as a tool, perhaps small and maybe misunderstood by some, to affirm a commitment of the local church to a local place? Even if the bulk of a church's membership doesn't live within walking distance of the building, the connection of those who worship there to the neighborhood can still be frequently and creatively affirmed. It seems more than incidental that the churches around Port William, in Berry's fiction, carry the very particular names of their crossroads settlements: Goforth Baptist Church isn't named for the Great Commission but for the store, school, and handful of houses of the village called Goforth. A name can be more than a label; it can be a commitment, a reminder, perhaps even a gift, if it points toward an actual narrative. To be given the name of one's grandparent is to be placed within a larger story; so also to be given the name of a place might allow a church to move more fully within the story of that place.

So if a church is named for a place and is at least potentially anchored by such an act, what next? Flipping Berry's critique of the church as ecological malefactor around, we would say that the church could and should become the leading steward of the ecology of its place. As a listening people, the church must be open not only to the cries of suffering people but also the groans of creation around us. Maybe it's better to say we need to be taught by the Spirit to hear the whole chorus of these cries together. This means more than ceramic versus Styrofoam cups at the Sunday coffee hour, and even more than building "green" church buildings, though such acts are not to be minimized, rare as they are. It means evaluating the livability and sustainability of a church's neighborhood: What is the ecology of the place, in terms of development of businesses and dwellings and parks? Who are the stakeholders, both positive and negative, within the neighborhood? What are the deep human needs, and what resources are available to meet them? We don't want the church to be an environmental club, any more than we want it to be a social work agency. But as a contributor to the healing of a place, a church must be aware of all the conditions of life, and of death, that surround it. The church has the redemptive word to offer, but to speak of our hope for the new heaven and new earth rings hollow when we ignore the sky above our head and the soil beneath our feet—and the neighbor on the sidewalk beside us.

The notion that local churches could lead the way in local ecology, stewarding both people and place, is a powerful manifestation of Berry's healing vision. I (Michael) have a friend who has carried such a vision through his college and now graduate work in environmental biology, with the specific aim of creating a resource organization to help local churches find ways to ecologically respond to their places. His vision sounds right, yet proves difficult to practice; hence whenever he and his wife come to visit our church in Grand Rapids, he doggedly volunteers to wash all the dishes after potluck dinners if only everyone will use porcelain plates and silverware (with which the church is mysteriously stocked) and shun Styrofoam and plasticware, at least for the day. To fellowship with Jonathan is to be pleasantly stretched and chastened!

The church of another acquaintance has traditionally been very involved in its local, inner-city neighborhood, forging solid bonds of racial reconciliation and social justice. Perhaps because of this openness, the church was able to bear an unexpected criticism from a local corner-store owner, who informed church leaders that their tradition of giving away huge numbers of Thanksgiving baskets in the neighborhood, the contents of which were purchased at a large grocery-store chain, was harming his business at one of the crucial sales moments of the year. The church not only heard the critique but responded by purchasing all the basket contents directly from him for the next Thanksgiving season. This story gives a twist on Berry's observation that food plays a central role in determining local health and connection: here a local church made a laudable adjustment to make a good ministry also a stewardship opportunity.

At a third level, a church that has named itself with respect to its place and has taken the lead in the stewardship of its place could also glean from Berry's "membership of Port William" a fuller understanding of what it means to be a member of a local church. Berry has taken a term historically associated with church (in more or less intentional notions of membership, depending on one's denominational affiliations or lack thereof), but his account of membership is almost wholly determined in the communal setting rather than the ecclesial. This is something more particular than citizenship, something not to be captured on a passport or any sort of paperwork. Yet it is a living connection, bringing a sense of belonging and also of knowing what you have to share and offer to the community. This ability to give, to offer back the gift offered, to invite even out at the margins, is the crucial denotation of membership, as we've argued in chapter 8. Here Berry's account, read back into the church, is a refreshing vision of what it means to belong within a church that is within a community. The dull and sometimes obnoxious conversation about the validity of church membership vis-à-vis voting rights, business meetings, and trusteeship suddenly can draw on a deeply rooted narrative of connections—past, present, and future. As an intentional member in a placed church, a person becomes sensitized to the practices and virtues involved in a shared life that moves from church to community to church in a dynamic loop. The centrality of hospitality and the ubiquitous nature of vulnerability and risk thus serve to guide the church's internal and external relationships. Indeed, the internal and external become a part of one another, membership *with* each other.

As Hannah Coulter recalls getting to know her eventual second husband, Nathan Coulter, after his return from the war, she reflects that part of her attraction was that "he wasn't *going* anywhere. He had come back home after the war because he wanted to. He was where he wanted to be. As I too was by then, he was a member of Port William. Members of Port William aren't trying to 'get someplace.' They think they *are* someplace."[9] What might such a realization mean in a church context? Rejection of mobility as a social

9. HC, 67.

norm for individuals and for institutions, as we've been arguing, is a life-giving response. Churches should not be easily persuaded to move because of population shifts and the promise of "prospering" elsewhere. Likewise, church members will not keep one foot always in the proverbial foyer, playing the field of various churches and looking for a "better fit" or "the next great thing." The disease of such fluidity is apparent even to the young people of today: in my (Matt's) church a survey of the youth revealed that their greatest desire was not an overhaul of worship styles or that the church in some other way reflect hip practices, but rather that they could find a place to belong. Berry's notion of membership suggests that a church can be decisively such a place, can live with a confidence that shuns the angst about who will stay or go from year to year. While certain strangers will come and go, never choosing to dwell with the church, a member can persist because he or she has fully received the gift of belonging somewhere and hence of being somebody, not just anybody.

There is a sobering side to this as well. For Berry, when a member leaves the community there is a dis-memberment that is as wounding and grim as that word suggests. In the threat of such dis-memberment, we recognize the risk of staying together in the light of the greater risk of being apart. The risk of our vulnerability with one another can be eased by the wrenching realization of what it would mean to leave and to lose each other. The language of 1 Corinthians 12, with its talk of the unified body and the coordination of its members, is very much in accord with Berry's vision, while the embodied consequences of its violation in the fictional world of Port William, the gaps caused by lost neighbors, wayward children, distant parents, and the press of forces external to the community, bring the horror of dis-memberment into sharp relief.

Clearly there are differences between Berry's discussion of communities and our discussion of churches. But the comprehensive nature of Berry's vision for life speaks to both, because he speaks to all of reality. Berry is no theologian: indeed he has no aspirations to be read as a theologian, and if we've done so we deserve

179

his censure! Only rarely does he speak directly to the church. But as Stanley Hauerwas has well articulated, Christians are called to be "truth-tellers,"[10] and that term seems to most fully capture Berry's purposes. So if we say that a holistic reading of Berry's works has shown to us the contours of the biblical worldview, that his poetry especially has sharpened our awareness of the goodness of creation and of the eschatological longing such goodness prompts in us, if we see in his critical essays an uncommon lucidity regarding the fallenness and idolatry of the world, if we glean from his fictional universe more than we can even articulate about the nature of living healingly in an already/not yet time, then we reveal at least a bit of the power of Berry's vision for our lives as God's people living out God's story in God's world. Inasmuch as the biblical story attests to the promise and the call to healing, Berry's work is a worthy and welcome retelling. And in telling the true story, he calls us beyond the narrow fables of our age.

What we've asserted here is not without controversy. In the November 2006 issue of *Christianity Today*, for example, Ragan Sutterfield's concise summation of Berry's importance includes several cautious voices. One of them is Richard Church, whose profile is a Wheeler Catlett-like "lawyer and farmer, with a PhD in theology from Duke," and who admires Berry's ideas but is anxious that "Berry is 'something of a Constantinian'—a cultural Christian who does not see a difference between the people of God and farmers in rural places."[11] Bolder yet is the critique made by one of our favorite curmudgeonly friends, Ralph Wood, who has a dual appointment in literature and theology at Baylor: "Wood finds in Berry a 'considerable kinship . . . with the Christian insistence that holy things will always come to us in communal and mediated form.' Yet he finds Berry's vision of nature Stoic rather than Christian—'everything fulfills its function by its *physis*, the principle of growth intrinsic

10. See especially Hauerwas and Willimon's *Resident Aliens: Life in the Christian Colony* (Nashville: Abingdon, 1989).

11. Quoted in Ragan Sutterfield, "Imagining a Different Way to Live," *Christianity Today*, November 2006, 63.

to it.' According to Wood, Berry misses the 'otherness of God' and settles for a deeply natural theology in which God's transcendence is absent."[12] Wood's concerns are not fully our own since his reading is more strictly theological. Sutterfield's quote of Ashley Woodiwiss, a philosopher at Wheaton College, better defines the tack we've taken, in both its peril and its promise: "[Woodiwiss] says we should ask, 'What does [Berry] have to offer us in terms of imaginative possibilities that Christians can really buy into?' "[13] As we hope we've revealed in this chapter, Berry offers not just pastoral analogies or environmental hints but rather a thoroughgoing vision for healing community that can help to create the "sustainable church" for each (and, we must pray, every) place and its people.

12. Ibid.
13. Ibid.

# 10

··············

# Sustainable Learning Communities

Since our reflections regarding the church are a first step toward applying Berry's comprehensive vision for healing to institutions he sees as diseased, then we'll take another step (at our own peril) by talking about education. If anything, Berry is more critical of contemporary education, especially the modern university, for its disconnect from local communities and abetting the corporate powers-that-be in their dislocating aims, than he is of the church. But we feel some impetus to look for healing possibilities, since, as with our involvement in local churches, we've already committed ourselves in the sphere of education. We both feel called to the vocation of teaching, and the classroom is the field where we sow and reap (we'll leave out any comments on the rockiness and drought-stricken nature of the soil at times!). If Berry's direct critiques of education are harsh, he is not alone in such censure; there is no lack of insights into the problems of the modern university; since Allan Bloom's salvo twenty years ago in *The Closing of the American Mind*, it has become almost *de rigueur* to render sharp criticism of the university's role in society. Few such critics have taken Berry's step of decisively quitting (though many have likely pondered it). But if the question is "Can education bring us home?" then we see Berry providing, in his broad strokes of hopefulness for healing communities, a pattern into which educational institutions can fit and offer good work.

As Berry sees it, the lack of boundary and limit is as much a part of the educational crisis, as it is of the political, economic, and agricultural crises. Indeed, these spheres begin to merge together as an unhealthy whole, with universities as both producer and product, spitting out graduates as raw material for the global economy. As universities become increasingly disconnected from the concerns of the people and places around them, they become more open to the influences of the peculiar spirits of our age: consumerism, technicism, hedonism. The students are abandoned to such ends even while on campus (this may have begun in kindergarten and is here only perfected) and aimed only toward such ends in their formal training and majors (or careers or skill sets or market-niches). Ironically, many large universities began with a sense of bounded purpose, tied to location and even to the land. One of Berry's chief laments regarding education is the loss of purpose of the land-grant university. In "Local Knowledge in the Age of Information," from *The Way of Ignorance*, Berry calls for the land-grant universities to enter anew (or maybe more fully) into genuine conversation with the communities they serve. The cooperative extensions that function as the embodied arms of the universities in rural communities (they are called local agencies) accomplish some measure of connection, but it is rarely the two-way conversation that Berry says will be essential for local places to flourish. Such nurturing will require far more involvement than just the placement of an agricultural biologist from the state university. Other aspects of the university, the local colleges, and maybe especially the local secondary and elementary schools must be considered in any plan for healthy community. Thus a prior need exists for all the elements of all the different educational institutions to learn to dialogue across boundaries, an activity sorely hindered by specialization. Education for the sake of creating producers and consumers for the global economy is a very different end from producing members for a healthy local community. What Berry makes clear is that educators can't do a good job at both aims—they are mutually exclusive. He laments that "the time is past, if ever there was such a time, when you can just discover knowledge and turn it loose in the world and assume that you have done good. This, to me, is a sign of the incompleteness of science in itself—which is a sign of the need for the strenuous conversation among all the branches of learning. This is a conversation that the universities failed to produce, and in fact have obstructed."[1]

Despite this dour tone, Berry has featured a few examples of such relational work in his essays, and these are worth mentioning. In his 1979 essay "An Agricultural Journey to Peru," Berry gives an account of one of his forays into a totally different cultural milieu. He did not leave without reservations: "For anyone with a farm, a two-week absence at that time of year will be problematical. For a raspberry lover to leave his raspberry patch at that time of year borders on calamity."[2] Among the attractions strong enough to usurp the raspberry harvest was Berry's connection to the Andean highland farmers: "Principally from the work of Stephen Brush, anthropologist at the College of William and Mary, I knew that this agriculture involved great skill and ecological sensitivity in the use of steep, rocky, and otherwise 'marginal' land."[3] In Brush, Berry found the sort of academician who could give space to his subjects and let them show their humanness, a very different angle from that of the cultural elite:

> Urban people, he said, generally assume that the peasant farmers are ignorant, that they have no systematic knowledge or method, that they don't understand the morphology of plants, that they name varieties whimsically or arbitrarily. He believes, on the contrary, that they have a great deal of sophistication in their choice and use of varieties and in their cropping systems. . . . This respect for the methods and intelligence of the peasant farmers is the foundation of his work, which thus opposes the destructive stereotype of the farmer-as-ignoramus.

1. LM, 145.
2. GGL, 3.
3. Ibid.

For almost a year he had been studying the use and cultivation of native potato varieties and local taxonomy, even growing some of the native varieties himself. He had spent many hours identifying and counting the varieties in various fields. As we talked, we had his complexly coded maps and charts around us on the floor.[4]

Brush's willingness to enter the fray of human issues, to be in a place with the people, such that a study becomes a lifestyle, is the sort of healing education that Berry admires and seeks to draw out wherever he finds it.[5]

## Responsible Education: Whose Responsibility?

When Berry's critique moves within the institutions themselves, by no means limited to land-grant universities now, he shows that an incoherence of scale and boundary is basic to the way contemporary education is structured and championed (in other words, funded). In *Life Is a Miracle*, he goes after the professionalization of education, whereby the motive in faculty development seems to be the creation of isolated "genius" and research, which "is always offering up the past and the present as sacrifices to the future . . . the utopia of academic thought."[6] At the very least, the role of teaching is sacrificed to the promise of research, since teaching "can't thrive in a cult of innovation."[7] This is an obvious breach of limit, because the university loses the student, except insofar as it serves by re-creating its own specialized types—a minority of "geniuses" to make up for the majority of students whose education has nothing to do with the culture they live in. School spirit becomes a function of athletic programs and fundraising campaigns, devoid of substance. The result is a kind of "academic Darwinism [that] inflicts severe

---

4. Ibid., 7–8.

5. Two other essays in *The Gift of Good Land* connect with this one: a few University of Kentucky professors are given good acclaim in "The Native Grasses and What They Mean," as is a host professor from Arizona in "Three Ways of Farming in the Southwest."

6. LM, 131.

7. Ibid., 65.

penalties both upon those who survive and those who perish. Both must submit to an economic system which values their lives strictly according to their productivity."[8] This systemic problem extends down to the lowest grades, where parents become obsessed with their children's biweekly test scores and the constant drumming of "mastering basic skills" invites the unavoidable, yet oft avoided, question "To what end?" Without any coherent human aims, education from kindergarten through college becomes a series of programmatic gestures, standardized tests, and obsessive activity, all of it culturally conditioned to grease the cogs of the global market with the next generation of consumer-producers.

In his most direct indictment of the role of higher education in the dismemberment of culture, the essay "The Loss of the University," Berry points directly to the deceptive specialization of academia, where the creation of manifold boundaries is in fact a reductionism that leaves only a false whole. These boundaries are not those that promote health, since the core function of the university, to create "whole human beings," is undermined. Here a revivification of core curriculum gets at the problem but can also be a kind of lip service to wholeness:

> The thing being made in a university is humanity . . . not just trained workers or knowledgeable citizens but responsible heirs and members of human culture. If the proper work of the university is only to equip people to fulfill private ambitions, then how do we justify public support? If it is only to prepare citizens to fulfill public responsibilities, then how do we justify the teaching of arts and sciences? The common denominator has to be larger than either career preparation or preparation for citizenship. Underlying the idea of university—the bringing together, the combining into one, of all the disciplines—is the idea that good work and good citizenship are the inevitable by-products of the making of a good—that is, a fully developed—human being. This, as I understand it, is the definition of the name *university*.[9]

8. Ibid., 62.
9. HE, 77.

But the unity for which Berry calls has been thwarted by a kind of double fragmentation. There is the loss of connection to the local community as something more than an anonymous neighbor to the school's premises and also the loss of internal coherence between disciplines and departments that might lead to the particular aim of fully developed human beings. Instead, what might be called the contemporary multiversity ends up creating diseased choices by mirroring the grocery-store aisle with one hundred varieties of cereal but nothing fresh and local. Instead of curriculum that helps anchor students in local concerns and possibilities, the consumeristic approach that students and parents have come to expect to augment their "private ambitions" leaves the students unsatisfied, because it points everywhere and nowhere, providing a gateway to a dislocated life. It is education as escape from community.

A university that is itself inhospitable—never locating students within healthy boundaries of community—will propagate graduates who cannot recognize or foster true hospitality. In "Higher Education and Home Defense," Berry has identified this end-product when he laments that one of the requirements for "entrance into the class of professional vandals is 'higher education.' "[10] Students are stunted in their growth toward full humanity by the very mechanisms provided for them as means of preparation. Then it becomes easy to seek solace in wired dormitories where they can play consummately inhospitable video games or "chat" on anonymous websites half the night. To pull off the mask here is to assert that "meeting students where they're at" really means diagnosing the diseased condition that most American young people arrive in as first-year college students—contaminated by boundless aspirations and flight from place. College is the culmination of twelve (or more, with preschool) years of training, but it is precisely the misdirected nature of that training that is perpetuated. All the rhetoric of the better life that awaits, somewhere beyond the intelligible boundaries that "confine" each student, and beyond the

10. Ibid., 51. See also the excellent article by Brian Walsh and Steve Bouma-Prediger, "Education for Homelessness and Homemaking? The Christian College in Post-modern Culture," *Christian Scholar's Review* 32, no. 3 (Spring 2003): 281–96.

known and knowable terrain of childhood and adolescence, ends up in an intense preparation for homelessness. It's not the case that today's students are less informed or are somehow devoid of skills; the real problem is that the end in mind is destroying them.

So our task becomes leading students toward health, a task that must be not only taught but also lived. Education isn't the only source of the problems, nor is it the solution by itself; educators cannot stem the tide of massive political and economic pressures. But it is a place where healing can begin, can be identified rightly and nurtured toward something like full flowering.

## Life-Giving Education

In order to effect such healing, the university community will be composed not just of placed people but also of placed ideas and traditions. There must be meaning and specificity in the values and ideas we propagate; the notion of a homogenous, cookie-cutter approach to "school spirit" should be just as heinous as such an approach to curriculum. To be incorporated into a tradition is not possible, because it's not a set of skills or practical applications. Instead, a tradition works like Berry's notion of "membership": it takes time and a certain amount of inconvenience to work. There must be invitation into the conversation, but students will need to receive the gift of a tradition's past meaning and present embodiment. Berry says in "The Burden of the Gospels" that to find important answers we must "be living and working"[11] at them for a long time. This requires an acknowledgment not of success and completion but of humility, of incompleteness and dependence on one another. This humility must be shared—the teacher opens up by sharing the tradition, and then the student becomes a cobearer of that tradition.

My (Matt's) annual harvest party with my philosophy students has served, over the years, as a way to invite students into a place and a way of thinking about rootedness and a level of comfort from

11. WI, 137.

which hermeneutical endeavors can flow. This is something of an extension, for me, of the hospitality-in-learning that I experienced as a graduate student at the Institute for Christian Studies in Toronto, where afternoon tea time facilitated the informal community that is necessary for scholarly endeavors to flourish.

This education is for the here and now within an unabashed eschatological vision of the future, again working in the spiral of that dynamic rather than the linear abstractions of futurists with their hard divisions between past, present, and future. Berry has often lamented the "futurist" tendency in American higher education as a breeder of dissatisfaction and dislocation. He writes in the essay "Looking Ahead" that "the future is the best of all possible settings for the airy work of academic theorists—simply because neither nature nor human nature has yet taken place there."[12] The problem for students is that their lives are always cast in future terms, which are diseased to the extent that they are abstracted. In this grand vision, classes become hoops and hindrances to something waiting up ahead, in the ephemeral future. Perhaps this is nowhere more evident than in the "information literacy" craze that has swept universities since the advent of laptops and iPods. Berry comments in "Local Knowledge in the Age of Information" about the deception bound up in this vision of literacy: "Let us consider how we have degraded this word 'information.' As you would expect, in-form-ation in its root meaning has to do with the idea of a form: a pattern, structure, or ordering principle. To in-form is to form from within. Information, in this sense, refers to teaching and learning, to the formation of a person's mind or character. We seem to be using the word now almost exclusively to refer to a random accumulation of facts. . . . There is nothing deader or of more questionable value than facts in isolation."[13]

The formation Berry hints at can come about only through humility and discipline, an acceptance of limits and boundaries as part of the gift of becoming fully human. These are the sorts of attitudes that

12. GGL, 177.
13. WI, 121.

the market deplores, because they militate against the illusions of autonomy that drive the market forward. They also militate against the culture of convenience and choice that is so deeply situated in the minds of most college freshmen. That inconvenience might in fact produce a far more sustainable way of life is the difficult idea we must champion.

So if we in the university set out to create an inefficient, inconvenient, humbling, bounded, and limited conversation, guided by an eschatological promise and lived out in a hospitable academic membership, then we're getting somewhere! In Berry's vision for a whole life of healing, this sort of education won't be enough, but it can cease to be part of the problem and can even allow the university to open up a broader conversation, one that includes local school districts, public and private (and home schoolers as well), within a bounded web of concern. Since we know the university best, and since the university trains those who will provide elementary and secondary education in every particular community, we'll concentrate our efforts here on showing how Berry's broad vision for life might help vivify and focus higher education in the near future.

## An Educator's Dream: Growing Students through Sustainable Education

Where does Berry point us? Our vision here is something we call "sustainable education."[14] We don't mean to limit the conversation to the initiatives in energy use, building practices, food purchasing, and campus landscaping that many schools have undertaken to foster "greener" and healthier settings. We wholly affirm these initiatives. These various proactive steps can be part of the sustainable setting we are aiming toward, but we're looking for a coherence that grows

---

14. We are both indebted to the work of Commenius, the seventeenth-century Bohemian educational theorist, whose works constantly use the agricultural metaphor for education—and our debt to Commenius comes via our debt to David I. Smith, whose work through the Kuyers Institute for Christian Teaching and Learning at Calvin College has been a tremendous benefit to us, and to many other teachers and scholars.

out of the human community, the "spirit" of the place, that will anchor the environmental practices.[15]

First, taking Berry's notion of all of life as a gift of God to be received and shared communally, we have to think about education as gift, given and received, never simply obtained or delivered. Instructors and mentors must thus be careful guides, vulnerable enough to admit they don't know all the outcomes of a seminar, despite the mandated use of learning objectives phrased in the scary parlance of "As a result of this class, the student will . . ." The mystery of each participant's particularity is the chief given, which thus undermines quantitative assessment as the end motive; this is not a contractual relationship, or even a horizontal setting where all are equal learners, but rather a loving, nurturing relationship. No one goes into education to ultimately have a set of assessment data in hand; we go in to see the "Aha!" and to reexperience the "Aha!" ourselves. Objective assessment can at best be only a partial way of measuring the success of a given class. We must also be willing to articulate and risk more human sorts of measures, which will cause us to be with the students, guided by their queries and interests even while guiding their growing sensibilities. If we're trying to throw a wrench in outcomes-based education, it's because we must ask, as Berry has done explicitly in one essay and implicitly in many others, "What are people for?"

A second notion we derive from Berry's vision is that the university has the potential to become a kind of workshop in membership, preparing students to help create and participate in healing communities once they leave. We recognize that this is almost the exact opposite of what Berry says universities now do, but here again, we will marshal his ideas as possible remedies for the woes he has diagnosed. Our hope is that education can slow young people down enough, can get in the way of "progress" for a slice of the formative

15. For a great account of what has been done and what might be done to create a "sustainable" setting for education, see the volume *Planet U.: Sustaining the World, Reinventing the University* (Gabriola Island, BC: New Society, 2006) by Michael M'Gonigle and Justine Starke, who use their homeplace at University of Victoria, British Columbia, as a model.

years, to let them see a "fully orbed glimpse of life" lived within a finite community.[16] Each graduating class then can resist breaking into hundreds of fragmentary, autonomous units and can instead send out visionaries and homemakers, attached to their university experience by ideas and relationships that are rooted in hope and the explicit promise of endurance. In "Higher Education and Home Defense" Berry ponders these possibilities:

> Education in the true sense, of course, is an enablement to *serve*—both the living human community in its natural household or neighborhood and the precious cultural possessions that the living community inherits or should inherit. To educate is, literally, to "bring up," to bring young people to a responsible maturity, to help them to be good caretakers of what they have been given, to help them to be charitable toward fellow creatures. Such an education is obviously pleasant and useful to have; that a sizable number of humans should have it is probably also one of the necessities of human life in this world. And if this education is to be used well, it is obvious that it must be used some *where*; it must be used where one lives, where one intends to continue to live; it must be brought home.[17]

Now, we assume that many of our students come to us already dislocated and disoriented because of the dysfunction present in homes, schools, churches, and communities. We could cite much anecdotal evidence to back up this assumption, as could most every educator in the modern world. Our first task, then, is to welcome, to offer hospitality that is not a token orientation program or a dorm-oriented, superficial network of acquaintances. Rather, we need to let students feel that they have found a *place*, perhaps for the first time, where they can safely evaluate, struggle through, and steward a set of ideas. The classroom setting, rather than being an addendum to community building on a campus, can lead the way

16. Taken from Douglas V. Henry's remarks at the After Evangelicalism conference, Cornerstone University, Grand Rapids, MI, September 2005, during a panel discussion on the future of the evangelical university.

17. HE, 52.

by showing a hospitable approach not just to relationships but also to ideas and questions. To wax metaphorical, the classroom can be a sort of dining-room table where the family gathers to discuss important family matters in a context of nourishment and pleasure. We don't spend all day at the table, but shared mealtimes are an essential part of a healthy household.

But a hospitable intellectual setting is not the end in itself; we need to turn around and prepare for the disorientation that will take place when a thoroughgoing biblical vision of life is offered—as Berry has phrased it, the "burden of the Gospels" will never fail to challenge us but will also never fail to orient us. So we have a hospitable disorientation afoot—what then? How do we build the trust that can allow for a kind of "wild space of love"? We must allow students to bring their questions and issues. One of the challenges of being a professor in Christian higher education is that one will spend as much time dealing with the messiness of students' lives as with the texts themselves. If fragmentation is the problem, then the fragmentation by which "expertise" keeps us all separate from the lived experiences of our students is not ultimately helpful.

The two of us have found that teaching together in the same class has helped us see some of the possibilities for such healing learning. The modeling of charitable discourse (most of the time) by which we lead the class and each other into conversation has a freeing effect on the students, who feel that if we can come alongside each other in dialogue, in spite of and maybe through disagreement, they can enter in as well. Over the past several years, we have taught such classes as Love and Friendship (along with a third colleague, David Landrum), Homelessness and Homemaking (a course clearly inspired by the Walsh and Bouma-Prediger article we cited earlier), and most recently Home Economics (a course rich in Wendell Berry readings, as you might imagine). Especially in this latter course, we very intentionally sought to help students locate themselves in a constructive way, to move toward a recognition of what it might mean to be at-home in their lives. Our final exam, a collaborative effort to create "Berryville," a sustainable and interwoven village wherein each student

194

took some communal role (whether running the local bookstore or pub, providing medical services, or renting bicycles and mopeds), was a lighthearted and insightful glimpse of what could be, and also why it isn't so easy. Our fictional community of Berryville was in a way merely a symbol for the deep connections that the students in this class began to recognize; the "fully orbed life" began to appear not so much in glances at another world as in realizations about this world, this class, taken together in the here and now.

The third challenge that we intuit from Berry's vision is to send students out to embody at-homeness wherever they will place themselves. This is the acid test for the work of Christian education: to see our graduates willing to do the hard work of "homemaking" in a culture that will constantly chafe against such a motive. How can the university help to sustain such efforts? Traditional alumni relations seem unilateral and almost purely fiscal, thus squandering the possibility of helping wisdom to accrue in an extended "membership." The increasingly ossified call to "homecoming" events, which seek to recapture an ambience or experience that alumni might recognize, point to the ambiguity of what "at-homeness" means to the university. Knowing that there will be a time, sooner rather than later, when the students will have to be "alone" with these ideas means that the community must exist as a substantive shared story that is more than just a function of proximity, either real or invented. This will call for a reinvention of what we mean by alumni. Can we begin to promise students that their education has equipped them to make a home for themselves in a place in this world? Can we promise them that they will continue to be part of the workshop, the training ground, for the fully orbed life, and that their struggles and successes in locating themselves will be part of a shared story, to help younger students and the dislocated and disenfranchised to renew hope and reenergize their work? We visualize the university as a sort of hub, where alumni are wanted not simply for money or word-of-mouth recruitment but rather for contributing to the ongoing project of helping create fully human, deeply rooted communities. This could work in some ways like a multigenerational family unit, where multilayered allegiances and shared wisdom and stories create a thick web that protects against dismemberment and isolation. Rather than being an end in itself, a university can become a complement to healthy local communities where the arts of living taught and modeled at the university are fully fledged by those who have learned them and seek to teach and embody them.

At present, the most affirming evidence for us that such a vision is taking hold at our university is to see a student go on to graduate school with the desire to return as a sort of junior fellow in the teaching ranks. Likewise, there is gratification in seeing students move into an inner-city neighborhood to live, teach, work, and embody some of the tenets we've opened up to them. Indeed, the broader vision that Berry suggests needs to be embodied in these and other difficult and risky connections. Foremost among them would be the possibility of alumni intentionally "relocat[ing] to abandoned places of empire,"[18] whether these be one's own rural community (and a small church and finite job) or some small village in Africa or megacity of Southeast Asia.[19]

At the heart of our proposal is a longing for a return to the more classic liberal arts, but we also see in Berry's diagnosis of the disease in the world an explicit call to arts of living that will directly address the particular issues of our time and place. Hence we see a responsibility to form students (or, to stretch Berry's phrase, to "in-form their characters") regarding their roles in economics and politics. So our fourth and final application of Berry's vision to contemporary education would be this urgent emphasis on both a politics and an economics that can reflect sustainable, hospitable relationships between communities and toward creation.

18. Rutba House, ed., *Schools for Conversion: Twelve Marks of the New Monasticism* (Eugene, OR: Cascade, 2005), xii.

19. A friend who works for Wycliffe Bible Translators in Southeast Asia, after reading his first few Wendell Berry books, asked me [Michael] and insightful question: "Is there is a place for the missionary calling in this argument of localism?" Insofar as Berry's call is to be a healing presence, at home wherever one finds oneself, we contend that this is also a vision for those who are called to be prophetic "strangers and aliens" in the world (for the Kingdom of God, mind you, and not for social mobility).

What Berry calls for in his essays, longs for in his poems, and embodies profoundly in his fiction is the possibility of "membership" for every person. This is a spiritual call and a philosophical call, but it is also political. Human beings living together in a place are inherently civic creatures. At some point, membership is practiced as citizenship, when a community acts in self-aware responsibility toward a common good that is internal and is also aimed to coincide with the good of other communities. There will never be universal agreement on what the "good" is, and pluralism is inherent in any society that holds within it a tension of competing ideas and interests.[20] The faithful local community is thus constantly challenged with the necessity of remaining vulnerable and generous even in the face of competing visions of the good.

The realities of a given place and context will always shape the notion of the common good, but the universal constant must be to not seek our own communal health at the expense of another community's health. Recognition of boundaries of health, rather than simply boundaries of economic and political possibility, matters immensely. The Darwinian thrust of the corporate forces leads to efficiency as the bottom line of a community's right to survive—"change for growth, or perish" thus becomes the watchword of local political and economic discourse. How can communities that want to seek a healing presence in the world even begin to turn the tide of massive political and economic pressure to surrender local identities and commitments, in exchange for the supposed security offered by the myth of the expansive regime/market? As our students enter the world, we'd like them to be equipped not so much with a set of answers to problems they've not yet even faced as with a set of meaningful questions that can help them begin to live as healthy economic and political members. Berry has often used the strategy of a list of guiding questions in his own essays, to provoke analysis and action without orchestrating every move. We might suggest further

20. Jonathan Chaplin has articulated what this "principled pluralism" might look like in his article "Rejecting Neutrality, Expecting Diversity: From 'Liberal Pluralism' to Christian Pluralism," *Christian Scholar's Review* 34, no. 2 (Winter 2006): 143–75.

that such questions, framed by Berry's vision, could help us move into the uncharted territory of what lies ahead. They might include these: How do local communities connect to one another, not just down the road but across the world? How might democracy work on so many levels at the same time? How can healthy trade and market activity take place in a world such as we live in now? How can we create mechanisms to provide for particularized needs in particular locations, without creating faceless bureaucracies or tacit displays of power? How do those called by justice intervene in violent locales? None of these questions have simple answers, obviously, but Berry's works might be a lively starting place to address them, because the vision for life and health stands behind what he has to say.

Perhaps we begin to see now that all the differing roles we fulfill—student, teacher, buyer, seller, citizen, worker, worshiper, eater, drinker, lover—give way to the hopeful call to be *members*. "Only the purpose of a coherent community, fully alive both in the world and in the minds of its members, can carry us beyond fragmentation, contradiction, and negativity, teaching us to preserve, not in opposition, but in affirmation, all things needful to make us glad to live."[21] Amidst our concern for the many different good things we all seek, we can find unity in the simple and profound recognition that we first need each other. In a given place, we must allow this need to guide our lives together, since apart and alone we would find ourselves as thoroughly uprooted as a wind-wracked tree. If politics demands a *polis*, a particular place with particular people, and economics demands an *oikos*, a household, writ small or large, then these realms of thought and action are best embodied in a community whose love for place and each other offers healing to its own members and those drawn into its life from afar.

With such a call to action ringing in the ears of his readers, Berry, like a good farmer and grandfather, sends us out now to learn the hard way, to put our hands to the plow and thus to figure out how hard it is to keep a straight path down the long, long row we are

21. WI, 77–78.

facing in our culture. We said at the outset of this book that Berry's vision, even when framed most critically, has always struck us as unusually hopeful. We now recognize this hope as grounded in the goodness of creation, a goodness that moves like ripples outward from the stone-drop of Genesis 1–2, through all the contours of human ordering and disordering, toward the "good end" at which Berry seems to squint with an old farmer's eye. Could it be that his squint toward life makes the vision that much clearer, that much brighter, so that one can stand to look straight at either sun or storm cloud, knowing that the universe turns in God's good hands all the while? Take up a Wendell Berry book, whether for the first or the hundredth time, and learn and keep learning such a squinting view of God's glory.

# Index

201